Pattern Design for Torchon Lace

Pattern Design

JANE ATKINSON

for Torchon Lace

B.T. Batsford Ltd · London

ISBN 0 7134 5242 0

Typeset by Servis Filmsetting Ltd, Manchester
and printed by
Anchor Brendon Ltd
Tiptree, Essex
for the publishers
B.T. Batsford Ltd
4 Fitzhardinge Street
London W1H 0AH

Contents

Acknowledgements

I am glad to have this opportunity of thanking all those who have helped and encouraged me during the preparation of this book. First, I must thank Gisela Thomas for allowing me to join her design course. Without her initial help I would still be floundering. Also important in setting my feet on the road to practical pattern design was the kindness of Nell Shelby, formerly of Bideford School of Art. Friends who provided impetus and aid include Dorothy Brown, who booked design classes for Poole Bobbin Lace Circle, and lacemakers Betty Wilson, Ann Dukes, Lin Allen, Alison Fenny, Jane de Pearle, and Sarah Weaver to whom my thanks are also due for continually widening and enlivening my researches.

I should like to thank Pauline Burbidge, David Pye and Eva Wilson who have kindly allowed me to quote or take illustrations from their publications. I am also most grateful to Jack Piper for his help over threads. Mary Hewson set me working on log grids, Bill Raymond produced wavy grids, and Barbara Smith and Jean Bullivant suggested and produced heat-sealed mats.

My family has been a constant source of support and advice, but this book would not have been written or produced without the help and hard work of my husband, Terry.

Introduction

Some people say that you cannot teach design. Modern practices are aimed more at opening up students' awareness to possibilities, rather than teaching them precise methods and theories. Certainly, design is a very personal thing, for we all see life in quite different ways and respond to different stimuli. It may then seem foolhardy to put one person's approach to design into a book. I have done so because many people are interested in designing their own laces, but are uncertain how to get started. Knowing the feeling only too well, I hope to explain and illustrate many easy ways to tackle the subject.

The traditional yard-laces (laces made by the yard) have always attracted me, yet there seemed something lacking – the really functional laces all had a similar look about them, and the really pretty laces seemed too delicate and time consuming to be functional. My feeling was that modern lace should embody all their good points – style, relative speed and a touch of luxury – but for a long time I had no idea how this could be achieved.

My chance came when I joined the design class run as part of our local City and Guilds Creative Embroidery course and – working with lace rather than embroidery – began to learn how to organize vague ideas into completed projects.

The more I worked, the more it became obvious that in order to make a good job of designing any yard-lace, we need to learn the basics of formal pattern design.

The old-fashioned view is that to do anything really well you first have to master the most basic of techniques. Otherwise, it is almost inevitable that one arrives at a point where further progress is impossible without going back to the beginning. This book aims to set out basic pattern skills in an orderly fashion that can be studied at the reader's own pace. It has grown out of a series of day-schools run for a local lace group, which originally gave me the impetus to apply design theories to practical pattern work on Torchon, the lace with which most beginners start. Without the classes, I would probably have continued to ignore a lace often considered too humble to bother with. In the course of exploring every avenue which could lead to something new and interesting, I have been surprised to discover that it has almost limitless possibilities – I hope they appear as inviting to you as they have done to me.

About This Book

This is not a book for absolute newcomers to lacemaking. Torchon is easy and quick to learn and it should not take long to master the techniques, with good books like *The Technique of Bobbin Lace*,[1] *The Technique of Torchon Lace*,[2] or *Torchon Lace for Today*[3]; or a good local evening class.

You need to be able to look at a pattern, and see for yourself roughly how it could be worked, in order to have the freedom to work out new designs. This does not mean you need to be able to do everything – as long as you know where to find the techniques you need, as and when they become necessary. You will find at least two other books useful – one on stitches[4] and another on techniques and finishing.[5]

The transfer of a motif to graph-grid is an essential first step for the translation of a new pattern into Torchon lace. Many of the diagrams in this book have been drawn on graph paper in order to familiarize you with this process.

If you feel put off by the colours chosen for my examples, use those which please you. Some of the samples have been made to fit with my home decor, and many others are purely experimental. I have tried not to dictate thread choice to you. By indicating only the size of thread used for each sample, the hope is that you may prefer to try something different.

You may have other solutions to the problems I have encountered, but I have tried to take a positive attitude. Much can be achieved if, instead of saying 'I can't do that', one murmurs: 'Now, there must be some way we can manage it!'

1 | Forward march

Whilst travelling abroad on Intermediate Technology projects, my father became adept at finding souvenirs to suit the family. So when he found a shop selling newly-made lace in Delhi, he just had to buy me some samples. At the time, he recalls, he did not think that I would find the patterns terribly interesting. What he had not realized, however, was that those Torchon patterns were identical to some illustrated in a lace dealer's catalogue of nearly a hundred years before (fig. 1), which I had just acquired.

This made me question why so little had happened to lace pattern design over those hundred years. Must Torchon lace always be based around such traditional designs? As the year 2000 fast approaches, should we not be trying to find new patterns, at the same time as preserving the old ones? And would not new materials and new patterns help to create new uses for our venerable craft?

Other craftsmen are trying hard to relate their wares to the world in which they live. Take the furniture maker John Makepeace: 'I don't believe in keeping dead skills alive for their own sake. I want to utilize those skills by making things that are useful now.'[1]

Skill is only part of the question. The birth of the Lace Guild in 1976 reflected a huge upswing in the popularity of lacemaking, and brought diverse techniques within reach of anyone who wished to learn them. But there is more to craft work than the revitalization of traditional skills. Mr Makepeace is lucky in that over the past century trees have not ceased to grow, nor have people ceased to need furniture. The hand lacemaker, by contrast, sees her best threads disappearing from the market, and knows that no-one now would dream of paying a fair price for her labour on a product the consumer has long lived without.

Indeed, over the past half-century new hand-made lace has ceased to have any market status at all. Lace mats and napery disappeared from the fashionable home after World War I, as twenties designers sought a clean, uncluttered and easy-to-run look for the ever-busier housewife. That smart homes again contain lace, many decades later, is due more to the boom in nostalgia than to a revaluation of its worth.

The cognoscenti may be prepared to place the proper value on a pair of Valenciennes ruffles which once took a full year to make, but in general, although the modern lacemaker is an object of slightly awed respect, her work is given little more than curiosity value. Some beautiful new Honiton and modern free laces are being made, but would not more contemporary-looking yard-laces help to improve the lacemaker's standing? The trouble is that hand-made lace is too often placed with 'folk revival' crafts, and is expected to fit an antique format. Lace well fits the category Melvyn Bragg describes as:

Crafts without the pressure of profit . . . things that take time to learn but can be learnt, that are difficult to do but can be done and in themselves have something of wonder when they are done superlatively well.[2]

Bragg undertakes an interesting examination of why people retreat into ancient crafts; possibly because they see that the industrial society no longer represents the answer for economic and intellectual survival. Perhaps those who enjoy making high quality products for their own pleasure even hold the key to the future?

There is so much to learn about the old ways of making lace that it can be tempting to stick with

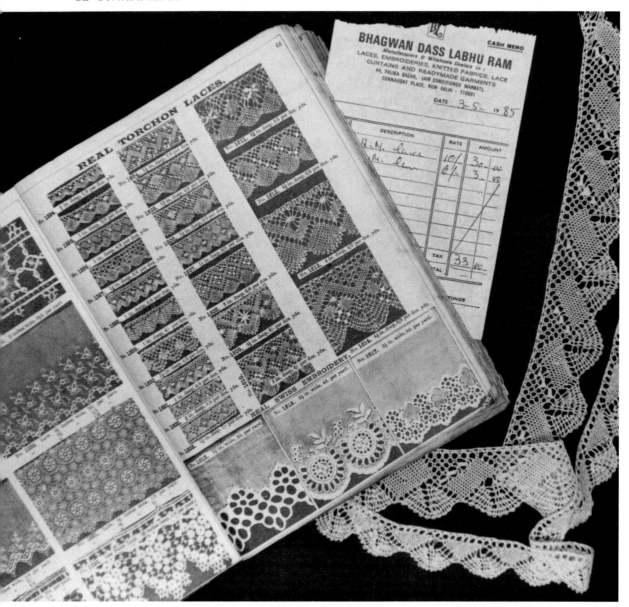

1 Nearly one hundred years separate the laces in the Samuel Peach and Sons, Nottingham, catalogue of 1896, and the new laces bought in Delhi in 1985, yet the designs are almost indentical. The prices are still woefully low – 10 Rupees per metre is only 60 pence, which includes the dealer's profit

the old patterns. Lacemakers are not normally people who let life slide by unchallenged, however – most are busy women who already organize a home, a family and a job, their feet firmly on the ground with lace as their absorbing hobby. One of the chief reasons why they do not produce new designs may be that pattern design is not the easiest of subjects to tackle alone and, so far, few designers have offered their help.

Another reason innovation is not immediately the province of the lacemaker is that history has

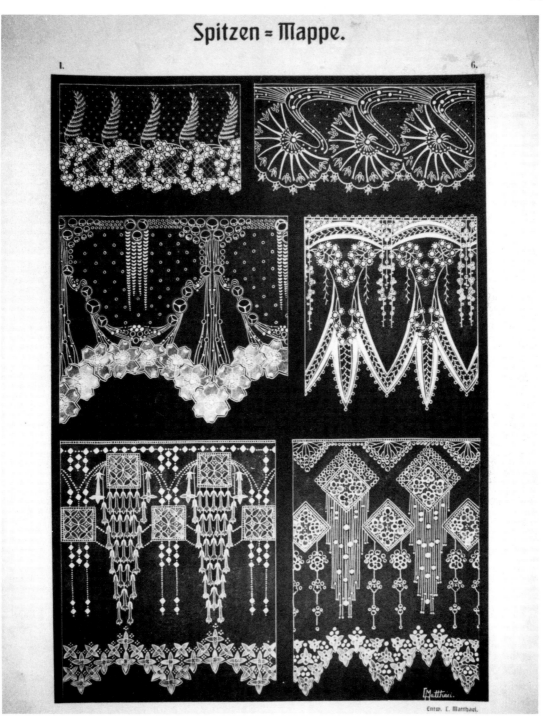

Spitzen = Mappe.

2 Art Nouveau (or the German equivalent, *Jugendstil*) lace patterns from the early years of this century, issued by Christian Stoll in Plauen for the commercial lace industry. The artist who designed this particular sheet (no. 6 of a book of 60), Leni Matthaei, took up bobbin lace about this time and went on to become one of Germany's foremost and most interesting lacemakers

not predisposed us to it. In reviving a moribund craft, practitioners have worked hard resuscitating old patterns and practices, but design itself has been all too often a male profession. And whereas other arts can look back to the late Victorian Arts and Crafts revival for inspiration and new design vigour, lace failed to keep pace.

One problem was that fashion at that time (and therefore the marketplace) demanded antique designs, and spurned the new. Torchon itself was a peasant lace, used by women who wanted sturdy household trimmings, and was worn with apology. My mother remembers her stylish aunt, music hall star Ethel Revnell, referring in disparaging tones to a 'nice bit of Torchon' – a term meant to denote lace so mundane, she would only use it to trim her unmentionables! Its makers would have had no incentive to destroy a fairly lucrative market, despite its low status, by thinking up new things to do. Some gorgeous Art Nouveau designs for machine-made lace were drawn up, especially on the Continent (fig. 2), but few went into production. The hand-made industry retreated into coarser and quicker patterns, and tended to rely more on the moral blackmail of protectionist do-gooders than on producing beautiful new work which could create a market of its own.

Some knowledge of lacemaking is needed before design can be attempted. One of the more interesting results of the Arts and Crafts movement was the journal *The Studio*, which not only featured articles about lace centres and designers (some glorious work was produced by the Imperial Royal School of Lacemaking in Vienna, and is well worth seeking out in Volume 27, 1902, p. 163) but also set lace design competitions for its readers.

These were not a success. The judges of the 1896 contest for a lace border were forced to admit:

The many drawings received are for the most part only of medium excellence. Messrs. Kirkbride and Co. of Nottingham, while admitting that a number of them are clever in design, are of the opinion that no single one has been entirely successful in catching the peculiar requirements of a lace design [fig. 3]. Many of them apppear to be more suitable for wallpaper borders

3 The first page of lace border patterns from the competition in *The Studio* in 1896

or stencil patterns than for lace, and it is probable that many trials must be made, even by the advanced designer, before he can hope to attain the exact conditions of a successful lace pattern. . . . We regret that we feel constrained to withold the first prize in the competition.

There might have been a ray of light if a few women had taken up the suggestion made by Mrs A. Penderel-Moody, in 1909, that lacemaking be left to women in poor agricultural districts who needed the money: 'the higher class worker must earn her wage by skill in such departments as designing, which the village girl is quite incapable of. It will need her quick wits and her good taste to keep the workers employed on up-to-date patterns, and she should be able to find a better market for the goods than they could possibly do themselves.'[3]

That the Honiton lace industry survived in better artistic fettle than the yard-lace industries further up-country is largely due to the efforts of a few talented individuals like Mrs Treadwin and Miss Trevelyan; but hand-made lace on both sides of the English Channel faded when World War I finally removed most women from their firesides, and set them on war work. One of the reasons put forward by the protectionists for keeping women lacemaking at home was to save them from the 'dangerous promiscuity' made possible by factory work![4]

Development continued on different parts of the Continent – it is well worth seeking out the work of talented designers like Leni Matthaei and Suze Bernuth in Germany, Dagobert Peche of the Vienna Workshops in Austria, Joannes Chaleye of France and Luba Krejci of Czechoslovakia. But their patterns have not crossed the Channel. It does seem that the result of this insularity in Britain is that hand-made lace is now often out of step with modern developments in the other textile arts.

Some query why we bother to make lace in the first place. On the face of it, only a fool would spend so many hours producing an article of little practical use, which serves neither to keep us decent, nor warm. Lace, however, has unique properties which make it an endlessly rewarding medium to explore. Unlike embroidery, it is freestanding and so can mix light and shade with its own textures and colours in a fascinating way; unlike mainstream weaving, each thread is infinitely manipulable, so the fabric is capable of immense diversity (using easily portable equipment). It can be produced in densities varying from gossamer to rope, with all manner of attractive threads, and the competition offered by industry is surprisingly limited. Despite its present low status, lace still means luxury to many, and in these stark and unembellished times it can offer an unrivalled source of ornament.

The subject of this book is not, however, lace in general, but geometric Torchon – chosen because it is the easiest lace to understand and make, offering the widest scope for both design and usage in different scales. The lessons learned in its design can form the basis of much work for other

laces too, and Torchon also has the advantage of being the most widely-made of the laces, worldwide as well as in Britain.

If one seeks to improve on the old Torchon patterns, perhaps one should first define why? Surviving Victorian patterns are limited in scope and number; they can be frustratingly slow to make; Torchon looks old-fashioned and out-of-step with exciting developments in other textiles, especially if always made in white or ecru thread; and old patterns often call for threads which no longer exist.

There is also the point raised by Susan Cox, Principal of the English Lace School, when she suggested to a Crafts Council lace study day in 1981 that if we do not produce new designs, no-one in years to come will be able to differentiate between the laces of the 1880s and 1980s. Much can be done about this situation:

* Patterns can be made to look more exciting.

* The scale can be enlarged to enable patterns to be made faster.

* We can use all the exciting threads the other crafts use and, moreover, mix them in a way other textiles cannot.

* Our lace can be made virtually any colour we fancy.

* It can, therefore, look just as modern as we wish to make it.

Most important of all, the lacemaker prepared to put in a bit of time in exploring the possibilities of her craft will regain that most important of all assets – *total control of the medium*. Patterns need not dictate the method of make-up and mode of usage – the lacemaker can have the freedom to choose exactly what she wants.

Faster lacemaking is important because our contempory society dictates that speed is of the essence; time is money. A craft which takes too long risks becoming an anachronism. Now that there is no longer the impetus to temper aesthetic considerations with commercial prudence, there is nothing to stop the lacemaker spending months on a beautiful but unsalable item. However, faster, bigger work with the same attention to quality and a more modern approach to design could, conceivably, produce items which again found a niche in the marketplace.

The other textile crafts are working at greater speed – home knitting machines are in wide use (would that there were one for yard-lace); patchworkers are machine-patching and quilting; embroiderers are exploring exciting machine projects (the lace garments of Robin Giddings, in machine embroidery on 'vanishing muslin', suggest we might throw away our bobbins here and now). The weaver Peter Collingwood has invented new ways of working: 'I decided I would have to make a rug every two days to sell at a reasonable price, so I had to find new quick techniques.'[5] All are making vibrant use of colour and texture. Fashions are ever more colourful – couturiers produce garments in coloured machine laces, and magazines glow with bright accessories. Lace is an important accessory, and does itself down if forever restricted to the colours (or non-colours) of the past.

Santina Levey, Keeper of Textiles and Dress at the Victoria and Albert Museum, told the London *Times* in 1984:

All the early lace had a purpose, and today's lacemakers have to think what is going to be done with the finished product and find a new approach to lace, using the old techniques to make new objects. This is what they are doing in Belgium and Scandinavia – three-dimensional sculptures for example, and pictorial panels in many colours.[6]

She is right about lace needing a purpose – but that does not need to be solely the creation of non-utilitarian art forms. There is heated debate these days on the place of functionalism in craft production – lace falls somewhere between the two extremes of visual non-functional art and utilitarian craft. The exciting field open to the lace designer is that of creating a new market for an item of which the public has hitherto been starved.

The art critic Peter Fuller showed that the designer who can make a good job of new pattern work does stand the chance of intelligent appreciation, when he wrote in 1982: 'The quest for good patterns, within the framework of developing but traditional craft practices, is still the most valid artistic statement which contemporary craftsmen and women can make.'[7] From Downton to Delhi, the call must be – what can we do about this?

Booklist

The following books contain inspirational 20th century Continental lace samples:

Leni Matthaei, ein Leben für die Klöppelspitze, by Inge Muhlensiepen, M. and H. Schaper, Hanover, 1980

Twentieth Century Lace, by Ernst-Eric Pfannschmidt. Mills and Boon, 1975.

Lace, by Virginia Churchill Bath, Cassell and Collier Macmillan, 1974.

Bobbin Lace, by Eeva Lisa Kortelahti, 1983.

Creative Design in Bobbin Lace by Ann Collier, Batsford, 1982

2 | Inspiration

When we first approach a design problem, one of the difficulties is that established traditions can cloud our vision. 'It is no easy task to discard conventions. Courage is an important factor in any creation; it can be most active when knowledge does not impede it at too early a stage', wrote weaver Anni Albers.[1]

We may need to stand back and take a more objective view of our own craft. Traditional Torchon lace could be said to be composed largely of diamonds, trails, spiders, fan edgings and decorative fillings, but exciting and individual effects are still possible if one looks outside this family of shapes.

A truer description of Torchon lace would concentrate on the fact that it is built on a four-sided, usually square, grid. Basic Euclidean geometry dictates that all regular patterns that repeat over a flat plane are based on three-sided or four-sided grids (or combinations of these grids). Five sides curve the plane (like a football) and six sides are just a multiple of three (forming the basis of the hexagonal mesh grounded laces like Buckinghamshire and Mechlin).

A rectangular grid appears far less versatile than a hexagonal grid – floral Torchon would be difficult and Flanders lace, which also uses a rectangular grid, incorporates various tricks to overcome the otherwise inhibiting regularity. Natural forms would need to be heavily stylized – an exciting area but not one I propose to cover here. (For some thought-provoking geometric stylization of plant forms, you might find the stained glass windows of the American architect Frank Lloyd Wright interesting.[2]) Furthermore, Torchon patterns are arranged on the diagonal, which restricts the use of vertical and horizontal lines. But there is still much to be done with it,

both by exploiting and by distorting its geometry (see Chapter 7).

Other media can demonstrate that Torchon lace is part of a large family of crafts utilizing rectangular patterns. Lace is, after all, an ornamental form of weaving, and there are many forms of conventional weaving, particularly primitive types, which use the fact that warp and weft meet at right angles to dictate pattern shapes. Early man started by weaving baskets to hold his berries, and very soon found he could ornament these by intertwining different coloured grasses into patterns. There are rectangular shapes in many of the crafts with which he then broadened his skills – weaving, fabric printing, floor mosaics, carving, even iron and glass work – which can inspire the modern pattern maker, particularly because of their simplicity and clarity (see fig. 4).

These distant avenues of decorative design are rewarding areas of study for the late twentieth-century lace pattern designer, for not only has her own tradition died out, but so has much of the tradition of ornament and decoration that used to be applied to both utilitarian and luxury objects used in everyday life; initially by the hand worker, and then in Victorian times to 'humanize' machine production. In contrast, the twentieth century has revered simplicity and plain, unadorned fuctionalism.

The pattern designer must be aware of past and present developments, for none of the decorative arts exists in a vacuum – architecture, furniture and industrial design, textiles, pottery or fine art all affect each other and form or follow society's taste. Lace in its eighteenth-century heyday both followed fashion and in its turn influenced fabric and wallpaper design; when looking for intricate

4 Geometric motifs from five continents
which can offer inspiration for Torchon patterns:
(a) North American Indian basket weaving;
(b) Egyptian weaving; (c) Melanesian textiles;
(d) Baluchistan textiles (e) Peruvian weaving;
(f) Pueblo Indian pottery; (g) Gothic strapwork

subjects for his virtuoso carving, Grinling Gibbons even included lace.

It must be no coincidence that lace has fallen into the doldrums in a century which has rejected the whole ornamental field of which it is part. Each succeeding stylistic movement is often a reaction against the one which came before it. If you think of the excessively fussy decoration of the Victorian era, you can understand why the Austrian architect Adolf Loos, writing in 1908, could call ornament a 'crime', partly from the viewpoint that the consumer was unprepared to pay properly for the labour that went into embellishing an object.

The early decades of this century saw a completely new attitude to art and design, with architects producing buildings to fit with the machine age, artists exploring sensory stimuli instead of sentiment, designers emphasizing form and function. In 1923 the Modernist architect Le Corbusier described the formation of a culture as the flowering of the effort to select, reject, prune and cleanse: 'the clear and naked emergence of the essential'. He went on to say:

Decoration is of a sensorial and elementary order, as is colour, and is suited to simple races, peasants and savages. Harmony and proportion incite the intellectual faculties and arrest the man of culture. The peasant loves ornament and decorates his walls. The civilized man wears a well-cut suit and is the owner of easel-pictures and books.[3]

Ornament did not die – designers at that time were indulging in a passion for a clean and simple geometry of which the Art Deco movement (a most potent source of interesting Torchon designs) made full use. Most of our towns still boast some useful Art Deco features on flats or cinemas. But hand-in-hand with succeeding styles has gone a steady streamlining of expression. Modernist architects have filled our cities with increasingly featureless, wall-eyed structures until people suddenly said: 'Enough!'

The new factor is that ornament is no longer a dirty word. As architecture professor Heinrich Klotz told the BBC TV series *Architecture at the Crossroads* in 1986: 'We have forgotten the measure of man; we have only asked for the measure of the machine. Suddenly we find out

that ornament, which has been disregarded completely, is something we need for man's soul.'

As well as finding a revived home in ornamental Post Modernist architecture, decoration is steadily re-establishing a higher status in the hand crafts. Pottery, for instance, for years followed the examples of pure oriental form made popular by Bernard Leach, but of late practitioners have also gone for some rich surface decoration. The irony here is that Leach himself was an artist with a great awareness of pattern, and wrote in his *Potter's Book*:

The problem of producing vital pattern is a very real one to the artist craftsman. He can no longer depend upon the support and restraint of any particular tradition but must form his own synthesis and invent his own creative designs, for pattern should rise out of the need and experience of today and not from that of yesterday.[4]

The ability to design vital (i.e. living) pattern needs to be cultivated, however. The most difficult way to work is to sit in front of a blank sheet of paper. All artists need to feed on beauty, whether natural or man-made, for the stimulation of their own creativity. The pattern designer, especially if designing for a specific medium, must add an awareness of the way in which past cultures have used the limitations imposed by pattern structure to create distinctive stylistic expression.

Past decorative styles have much to teach us; pattern for the primitive craftsman (and not-so-primitive craftsman) was not just ornament but a language, embodying symbolic or ritual elements. Certain basic geometric shapes appear in many cultures. Christianity used the sun circle, for example, in the glorious medieval rose-windows to proclaim eternity and unity, while concentric circles in African Ebo body painting also portray life and continuity, said to be derived from the tendrils of the yam. The 'Christian' cross may be equally significant to pagan worshippers in other cultures – for the Andean Peruvians, the cross was the symbol of a major festival held each year to celebrate the appearance of a constellation thought to herald dry weather.

As well as giving significance to shapes, symbolism helped to guide colour choices. Again, we may be most familiar with the symbolic use of colour in the Christian Church (red for Pentecost, purple for Advent, green after Epiphany); but Horuba bead workers in Nigeria might choose blue and gold to represent one god, and red and white for another. Colours may have opposite meanings in different cultures – to the Japanese, black means joy and white is for mourning, one reason why the Orient was slow to accept lace, as Mrs Bury Palliser pointed out in 1875 in her *History of Lace*:

Acting Consul Trotman reported from Hangkow that a large quantity of hand-made lace is made in the Roman Catholic orphanages there, but this was entirely for European consumption. White lace in China is not woven by the natives, for white and blue being the national mourning colours, and severe simplicity of dress being de rigueur on these occasions, lace of these colours has no sale.

Bereft for the most part of mystical significance, colour must now be used theoretically or intuitively. Symbols still abound in commercial life (as logos) and in communal life (such as street signs), but it is a moot point how many of these we would wish to transfer into lace.

Another important feature of primitive pattern is its sheer inventiveness. The designer will get the best results by 'playing' and experimenting, without worrying whether he is, in fact, 'reinventing the wheel'. An important influence on twentieth-century design was the Bauhaus, the art school founded in 1919 in Germany by the architect Walter Gropius. Here students were taught to experiment, to play, to think. One of the teachers, Joseph Albers, wrote:

Our aim is not so much to work differently as to work without copying or repeating others. Sometimes the results of experiments represent innovations in the application or treatment of material. But even when we evolve methods which are already in use, we have arrived at them independently, through direct experience, and they are our own because they have been rediscovered rather than taught.[5]

There are vast resources at the disposal of the pattern-maker, but one of the first questions she will need to ask herself is what to use them for. Walter Gropius described design as giving life and shape to your inner vision – we may have a vague

idea that we want to design something different, but no concrete notion of precisely what form that should take.

The most basic need is to cultivate an open-minded awareness of what really appeals to *you*. Instead of heading straight for the lace section in, say, the Victoria and Albert Museum, try wandering through the sections devoted to other applied arts in this vast melting-pot of cultures – and work out what really makes a personal appeal. You might be waylaid by the colour possibilities offered for lace by an Islamic mosque lamp enamelled in blue and gold on translucent glass; or the effect gained by Venetian glassmakers with their 'vetro da trina' – in which milky patterned canes are fused to produce objects which look like frozen lace – or the unusual colour combinations of a Chinese vase; or the gold filigree enamelling on granular grey French porcelain.

Special exhibitions often offer much food for thought, for all pattern is grist to your mill. Long established firms may offer retrospective displays of wallpaper or furnishing fabric designs; museums may offer textile or pottery collections. Organizations like the Crafts Council may bring an exciting show of Russian design or the Commonwealth Institute a display of Peruvian textiles –keep an eye on the newspapers and make the most of these fleeting opportunities.

Newspapers can also keep you abreast of design thinking, architectural controversy and fashion shifts. Look out too for specialist publications like *Crafts* magazine; visit the Crafts Centre and the Design Centre to evaluate trends. One of the most controversial new buildings in the City of London is the Lloyds building designed by Richard Rogers and his team – it is a 'high tech' construction full of light and shade, grain and shadow. Fig. 5 shows a pattern inspired by the building's most striking feature, the stainless-steel-clad stair columns.

The local library should be scoured for books on decorative history (seek out Owen Jones's *The Grammar of Ornament*, published in 1856 but republished by Studio Editions in 1986, which is a real treasure trove). Glossy magazines are an ideal source of inspiration (the more expensive, the more beautiful the contents). Start a scrap-

5 The controversial Lloyds of London building brought striking grey and silver geometry to the City skyline. The stair towers offered an unusual shape which fitted well into a circular pricking, and would be interpreted in alternate bands of silver (DMC *fil d'argent à broder*, two semi-fine threads per bobbin) cloth stitch, interspersed with bands of grey half-stitch (Bockens 16/1 linen)

book – a gardening feature might offer a particularly pretty and unusual colour combination, which you could use in your work at some point. Plants in the garden itself can offer ready advice on colour and form. Take note of what you see; use a camera if you have one handy to make a record: analysis of colour combinations and proportions will prove of real benefit. Beautiful

winter patterns in snow and ice may cry out to be transferred into lace. The more experience you gain in *looking* and appreciating, the faster will flow your ideas.

The woodworker and teacher David Pye described the process in his book *The Nature and Aesthetics of Design*:

The artist has glimpsed something: he has seen, perhaps fleetingly and indistinctly, some particular relation or quality of visible features which had previously been disregarded and which impressed itself on him by its beauty. By means of making a work of art, he then seeks to fix, isolate and concentrate what he has seen . . . All good works of art look as though they came easily. In a certain way they look obvious . . . What the artist does is not to create but to discover, isolate and concentrate . . . What the artist discovers, isolates and concentrates, he usually becomes conscious of and expresses in an entirely different context from that in which he first sighted it. A designer designing a tool may give it a profile which derives from something he saw in a mussel shell, or in a turbine blade, or in the lift of a road over some particular hill, or all three.[6]

Finally, here is a quotation from Krome Barratt's *Logic and Design*: 'It is not possible to predict the unimaginable. Therefore, any expectation is a projection into the future of past experiences or a combination of past experiences.'[7]

The more you come to see lace as one corner of a vast field of design problems – with not just its own answers but answers that can be borrowed from across the spectrum of media, taste and time – the faster will flow the ideas for the creation of new laces, and just as importantly, new ways of interpreting the patterns you create. Recent textile design has tended to stress geometric pattern – the time could be ripe for a Torchon revival.

3 | Materials

The good craftsman takes pleasure in organizing himself and his tools, and in using the best materials. Good work is made so much easier when everything is ready to hand, and you can trust your materials to deliver the results you require.

Somewhere to work

Many of those attempting their first lace designs will be busy housewives, so it is worth making the point that design cannot be properly enjoyed on a corner of the table between stages of bread-making. You owe it to yourself to find a quiet corner of the house where husband, children or grandchildren know to leave you in peace, and where Mum's pens can be trusted to remain undisturbed against the next half-hour she has free and can return to her design project.

It will be too much to expect most homes to accommodate a full-size drawing board, so useful for large items and the inevitable mess-making, but a small board or the old kitchen table would be a great help.

The right equipment

If you are serious about design, equip yourself with:

* Pencils – the wooden pencil constantly needs sharpening. Much better is a modern propelling pencil with automatic lead advance: one with 0.5mm 2B leads will give a consistently fine, dark and ever-sharp point.

* Erasers – remove pencil mistakes with a good rubber: a long, thin pencil-shaped one like the Staedler Mars-Rasor allows clean, accurate work. Pen errors can be blotted out with a proprietary typing correction fluid such as Tipp-Ex.

* Pens – there are many fine-point draughts-man's pens on the market; some use a hollow metal tip (which clogs); some use a fine fibre tip (which wears down); others now have a ceramic point. Most of the patterns in this book were drafted with a Tombo 0.18mm fibre tip. There are also many excellent 0.5mm throwaway versions on the market.

* Prickings – patterns can be drafted in pencil on graph paper or on tracing paper over a special grid, the final pattern being traced off in ink. This can be photocopied and the copy can be covered in plastic book-covering film such as Libra-Protecta Seal, best backed with a piece of fine card like Bristol board. Medium weight pins can then be pushed straight through the dots on the pattern (although you do bend some). All the materials can come straight from the local stationers, and such patterns have a long life – for fine patterns, a good backing material is the thick paper used for watercolour painting, which is kind to fine pins. There is thus no need to prick out or mark in patterns, although some teachers do feel this is a necessary stage in the knowledge of one's pattern. You may find it easier, especially if your eyesight is troublesome, to prick patterns through first.

* Paper – tracing and graph paper should be bought in the largest quantity you can afford; you do not want to feel inhibited by lack of materials. Most of the patterns in this book have been drafted

on $\frac{1}{10}$in or 2mm graph paper, but more unusual grids are discussed in Chapter Seven.

* Photocopiers – a girl's best friend is her photocopier. The modern machines will enlarge or reduce patterns, which gives you marvellous flexibility. One versatile pattern can be made up in thick coloured linen or the finest silk, if you get to know how many times to enlarge or reduce a pattern for the thickness of your thread. The only trouble with a photocopier is that it will distort patterns slightly – if reducing a pattern with a corner, the dots will come out at slightly different distances apart in the vertical from the horizontal. However, you can then cut the corner in half, and mirror one side only for a perfectly symmetrical pattern.

* Drafting tape – when tracing a pattern, it is hard work to have to hold down your tracing for a long time. Either work on a clip-board for small patterns, or tape larger pattern pieces securely with drafting tape. This looks like masking tape, but is easier to remove afterwards.

* Drawing aids – be careful if you try to use a ruler when drawing pattern shapes, as it is all too easy to drift from the desired line.

6 Pattern drawn on $\frac{1}{10}$in grid, useful for experimenting with texture

Materials

The current range of lace threads is very restrictive. Most are produced only in white, and, although the Swedish lace linen (and the Irish) is spun in its natural colour, few stockists supply it. Linen is also very hard to dye, needing a good long boil in the dye-bath. Much of the thicker cotton thread used for bobbin lace is not bobbin lace thread at all – DMC *fil à dentelles* is tatting cotton, rather springy for work under tension and inclined to shrink out of shape when the tension, produced by the pins, is removed. Cordonnet is crochet cotton, with similar properties. These two at least have the advantage of being quite cheap, but linen thread is not, which can be inhibiting to experimentation. Cotton thread can also look rather dull.

It seemed necessary to find some economical threads which could cope with bobbin lace tension, allow the use of colour and enable texture to be added. Lacemakers looking for new threads often turn to embroidery for inspiration; far closer to their medium is weaving, where some very useful threads can be found. It is suggested that the yarns described below would be suitable for the main grids used.

1/10in

Lace thread already used: DMC *fil à dentelles*, Bockens linen 40/2, 50/2, 60/2, Campbells linen 50, 70.

Linen – 16/1 Bockens Lingarn from Holma Helsinglands AB of Sweden (see stockists) who also spin the equivalent lace thread. This comes in 52 colours, with guaranteed colour-fastness to light and washing, and also works well in $\frac{1}{8}$in or larger grids (such as $\frac{1}{10}$in and $\frac{1}{8}$in blown up once). Disadvantages are that it is not as smooth as lace yarn, and, being a single thread, can snap in weak places. Care and experience will overcome this (extra strength can be added by twisting weak spots), and the resultant lace is very useful for furnishing or heavyweight dress use and has linen's crispness and lustre. Bought straight from the importer, it can be a quarter of the price of lace linen.

Silk – 40/3 super spun silk from Hilary Chetwynd. This produces a soft furnishing or dress lace which makes the most of silk's incomparable lustre.

Cotton – Bockens Bomullsgarn 16/2, also from Holma-Helsinglands, in 60 colours. This is softer, duller, and rather limp in comparison with the linen, but very strong and drapes well in dress use.

2mm or smaller grids

Lace threads already used: Swedish linen 80 or 90, DMC *retors d'Alsace* 30.

Silk – 300/4 silk from Jack Piper of Suffolk. This makes use of the wonderful lustre of embroidery floss, only very lightly spun to hold the filaments together. Available in white or a range of brilliant colours, this makes a delicate lace. Disadvantages are that it can easily catch and pull in rough usage, and needs a larger than usual number of pins left in to hold it in shape as you work (or threads will pull from quite a long distance). Advantages are that this was the nearest I could get to the thread used for the old Maltese lace, which has proved over the past hundred years to be a born survivor. Nothing can touch it for beauty, soft drape, or versatility. Workers and passives in contrasting colours will 'shoot' like shot silk; in a tight corner the thread reduces to nothing instead of bunching, spreading out evenly where more space is allowed. This makes it ideal for patterns using a circular or varied grid (see Chapter Seven).

Nett and spun silk, in various grades, are also available from Mr Piper, the former particularly bright and lustrous, the latter produced in a good range of colours, but duller in texture.

Guttermans 100/3 embroidery silk, from Doreen Holmes and D.J. Hornsby, is a spun silk in a fabulous range of colours, but needs to be handled with a little care. It works well, but has been known to snap at the knot in finishing, so you need to know exactly how much tension to apply.

Very fine grids

Lace threads already used: DMC *retors d'Alsace* 50 or 60.

Silk – 90 denier silk from Jack Piper, in the same colours as the 300/4. These two threads can be used together in a light lace to give a heavier contrast trail or motif.

Cotton – Mettler no. 30 machine embroidery thread makes fine trimmings in a wide range of shades, which is also very useful for cheap colour experimentation. Coats Trident 60 mercerized, which is fine, strong and even, also comes in a reasonable range of colours.

Textures

While most textured yarn is too thick, even when split, to be used for a whole lace, it can be mixed with a finer, smoother thread by using just one worker thread in a textured trail, instead of two.

The pattern offered here (figs 6 and 7, and plate 6) was designed for that purpose, and can be used for experiments (it grew from a desire to see if Torchon could work in irregular, abstract patterns as well as formal geometric designs). Try the main body of the lace in coloured linen or silk, with one central textured worker. The problem with recommending specific texture threads, many of them bought from knitting shops, is that they come on and off the market so quickly. If you cannot find these, seek suitable substitutes.

∗ Textured knitting yarns (with a good linen content) such as:
Yarnworks Potpourri (split into its two component threads)
Berger du Nord wool/linen, split
Filpucci Graffio, viscose and linen (good in $\frac{1}{10}$ in patterns blown up once, see plate 6).

∗ Tussah slub silk, and super spun silk 9G from Hilary Chetwynd.

∗ Raffene (split in two).

∗ Metallic threads such as:
DMC *fil d'argent a broder*,

DMC *fil d'or*,
Springer Goldfarden (metallic and lustrous viscose).

All sorts of threads deserve to be tried – the key is to experiment, for this is the only way you will learn and discover new things.

Thread charts

When you start experimenting with new threads, combing shops on your travels for interesting additions to your repertoire, it can at first be difficult to decide whether a thread has the properties you are looking for. A thread chart, containing little bits of yarn with which you *are* familiar, will be useful: carry it in your handbag. You will then be able to make a quick comparison of thicknesses with a new thread.

Test a new thread for strength – bobbin lace thread needs to be strong so that it does not snap. Ideally, it should not stretch at all; make sure that it is not too springy.

Bobbins

I have purposely restricted patterns in this book to those which can be made up with spangled bobbins. However, the use of Continental bobbins can bring a new dimension to lacemaking. The bigger Continental bobbins allow the use of thicker thread, which, when used with wider grid patterns, can bring the reward of faster and more exciting lacemaking.

Colour

Colour is a commodity to consider like any other, and offers great fun – it seems such a pity lacemakers do not use it more. Modern homes can take bright trimmings even better than white ones, and coloured laces also make lovely dress trimmings, quite apart from non-functional art forms.

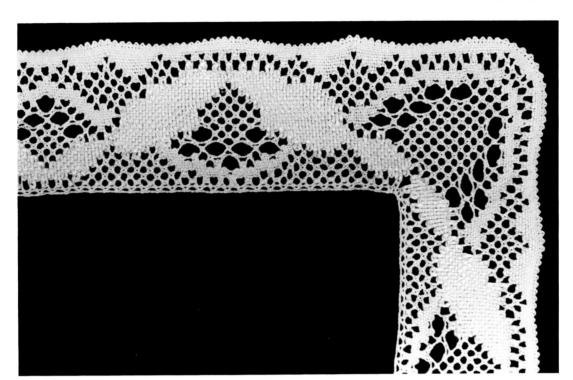

7 Texture pattern worked in 40/3 super spun silk, with the central motif in one thread of super spun silk 9G (see also colour plate 6). 24 pairs plus single texture bobbin

But those new to colour may need help – perhaps one of the reasons why coloured thread seldom caught on in the past was that it was often mixed (in yard-laces) with white, which kills it. The answer is to be bold, as long as the use of colour is carefully thought out and controlled.

We perceive colours by their relationship with adjacent colours – orange thread on a red background, for instance, may appear yellow, and against yellow may appear red. So it is important to make the correct choices if we are to mix coloured threads, or to trim a dress of one colour with lace of another.

The best course is to learn some colour theory. An influential teacher at the early Bauhaus was Johannes Itten, whose book *The Art of Color*[1] still cannot be bettered. What he has to say for painters is equally interesting for lacemakers.

You will find it useful to get to know the colour

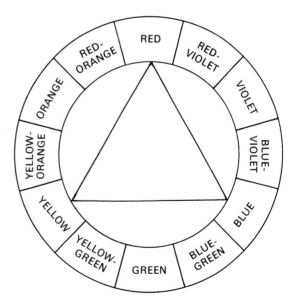

8 The colour wheel

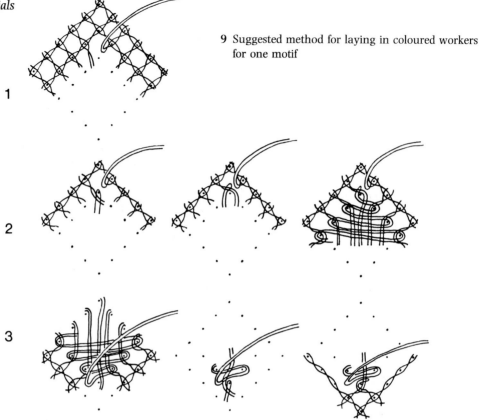

9 Suggested method for laying in coloured workers for one motif

wheel (fig. 8). There are special relationships between:

Primary colours – red, blue, yellow.

Secondary colours – orange, violet, green.

Tertiary colours – such as red-orange, orange-yellow.

Complementary colours – at opposite sides of the wheel (like red, green).

Split complementaries – combinations of the colour with hues on either side of its complement (such as blue, red-orange, yellow-orange).

Analagous colours – those side by side on the colour wheel (red, red-orange, orange).

Double complementary pairs – such as yellow and yellow-orange with violet and blue-violet.

Triads – three colours equidistant on the wheel (like the primaries).

Tetrads – these form squares or rectangles on the colour wheel (such as yellow-orange, red-orange, blue-green and blue-violet).

The interweaving of coloured threads presents a host of new experiences for the lacemaker, who will have to make her own rules. The most useful place for guidance, in fact, is a good book on weaving, like Ann Sutton's *The Structure of Weaving*[2] or Else Regensteiner's *The Art of Weaving*.[3]

In the colourist's jargon, tints are the basic hues mixed with white; tones are the hues mixed with black. When you mix coloured threads, white will deaden a bright colour, and black will intensify it; a neutral may best enhance its true value. Two bright hues will tone each other down; a small quantity of a bright hue with a larger quantity of a dull complementary (especially bright red and dull green) will increase in intensity and will further deaden the dull one – an effect known as 'zing'!

However, lace is even more complicated than weaving, in that one is already using light, shade and texture, and too many colours may dissipate the impact that might have been gained by a more restricted palette. A two-coloured lace (and two colours are often quite sufficient) may also need special selection of a third backing colour to give correct emphasis.

Tudor portraits show that bobbin lace *started* in colour – so white is not sacrosanct. It is important that lace should possess the ability to respond to fashion if needed; recent trends have been to bright primary and secondary colours, and to pretty pastels. You will be ruled by personal taste, but a knowledge of colour theory will help you get the most out of your preferences.

Colour mixing

If you have not mixed coloured threads before, perhaps we had better discuss how to mix them. You can:

∗ Use the edge worker pair in a different colour.

∗ Use a different coloured worker in a continuous trail in the middle of the lace.

∗ Hang in a different coloured worker to make a simple motif (i.e. one that does not divide and thus need two workers).

To do this (fig. 9):

1. Hang out the passive pair that would have become the worker.

2. Hang the new coloured pair on the first pin of the motif; work a whole stitch with the other passive; take the pin out and put it back in the hole, between the two pairs, and enclose it with another whole stitch.

3. At the end of the motif, work a whole stitch; hang out the coloured worker; hang a new base-colour passive on the last pin and work a whole stitch with the other remaining passive; take out the pin, replace it between the two pairs and enclose it with a whole stitch.

4. Secure the pairs you have hung out, while there are still some pins in to stop the threads pulling. Sew in the top pair, and knot both pairs off – I sew the ends in, and the result is both neat and secure.

∗ Use a contrast worker to make a series of adjacent motifs so the thread runs from one to the next (see fig. 20). The easiest way to do this is to *cheat* – or the coloured threads will not be in the right place each time.

1. The coloured worker from the first motif is worked to the intervening pin in whole stitch, then to the next starting pin. Either, (a) change the direction of the worker (as in photo frame, fig. 151) or (b) cross the worker and passive in whole stitch, then switch the pairs over in your hands, put up the pin and enclose it with a whole stitch – the coloured threads from the first motif will then be ready to work the second motif and the changeover will not be obvious.

2. If working round a square or oblong, incorporate a back-stitch in the centre of each side and the threads will come exactly as you want them at the start of each side.

3. If using a thick metallic thread, as in the coaster (fig. 149), the easiest thing may be to work the first pin hole of the next motif as half stitch, pin, half stitch, then carry on as normal.

∗ Hang in groups or bands of coloured passives, either controlling their progress or letting them meander. This can be rewarding, but may demand careful planning.

Techniques

One final tip may be useful. A student once asked me: 'Does it matter which way you draw in trails or motifs? Left to right, or right to left?' My answer, after some thought, was that I could not see that it mattered, as long as one was consistent – which I have tried to be in this book.

However, if you look at zig-zag trails you will notice that they become thinner in one direction and thicker in another; in half stitch this even means an extra thread travelling along the motif. You can make use of this, to increase or decrease contrast, by incorporating a back-stitch, or working short trails in a different direction (as was done in fig. 78 to thicken the trails).

10 The chevron motif is easy to work from any
direction (this diagram also shows how to join
and divide trails)

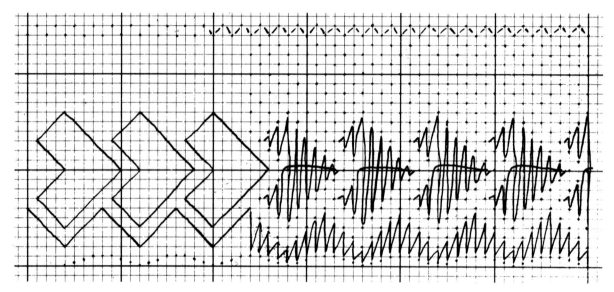

11 Motif pointing from left to right. (Trace for
pricking)

4 | Pattern practice

Most of us begin our designing by doodling on a sheet of graph paper, but soon realize that we need to be more organized. If we now examine some of the basics of border pattern design, we can then apply this knowledge to create simple laces.

The Victorian pattern designer Lewis F. Day wrote in 1887:

'The popular idea of the process of ornamental design is, that the artist has only to sit down before a piece of paper and, like a spider, spin out the fancies that may crowd his fertile imagination. Indeed, there is scope in design for all his fancy; but he is no Zeus that ornament should spring, Athena-like, full-grown from his brain.

12 Pattern made up in DMC *fil à dentelles*. 28 pairs

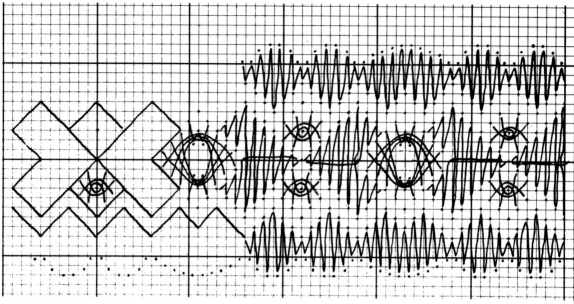

13 Eyelets divide the motifs

Ornament is constructed, patiently (I will not say laboriously, for the artist loves the labour), patiently built up on lines inevitable to its consistency.[1]

This is a good point – I feel that far too many people think, because they cannot instantly dream up a new pattern, they are no good at design. The notion that genius is ten per cent inspiration and 90 per cent perspiration is much nearer the truth.

Since all the patterns in this book result from a search for variety, we can use them to illustrate certain basic points of pattern design:

∗ *Pattern* is the repetition of one or more elements, united by *rhythm*.

∗ This rhythm may be *rigid* (fig. 38) like much Torchon design, or *fluid*, as when graded grids are used (fig. 78), or circular ones (fig. 40).

∗ *Stop* patterns offer their elements in staccato fashion (fig. 49d), but even a rigid pattern can flow, if one's eye is led on from one element to the next (fig. 102).

∗ Patterns may be *vertical, horizontal* or *diagonal* – Torchon poses the problem of how to produce vertical or horizontal border patterns from predominantly diagonal elements.

∗ *Emphasis* may draw the eye to a particular part of the pattern, such as the top (fig. 140) or the bottom (fig. 26).

∗ Elements may be *symmetrical* (fig. 57) or *asymmetrical* (fig. 87), *regular* (fig. 91) or *irregular* (fig. 61). But lace patterns which may need to be worked several times over the same pricking will need some, probably marked, degree of regularity. (Symmetry itself can be in vertical, horizontal or diagonal planes, or arranged round an axis – the figure used later in this chapter is asymmetrical in one direction, but can be cut into two symmetrical halves in the other direction.)

∗ Patterns can also be *naturalistic* (fig. 3), *Abstract* (fig. 7) or *geometric*. Torchon is not easy to use in naturalistic fashion, so this book attempts to make the most of what geometry has to offer.

∗ Lace is one of a select band of media which incorporate *light* and *shade*, and needs plenty of light and dark contrast to give it life. But these elements may work in different ways according to the way the lace is to be displayed. Thick, cloth-stitch areas may appear light on a dark background, or dark against a light background.

In all the design books I have read, only one mentioned lace; this was *Practical Designing* in which Arthur Silver wrote:

14 Bockens 16/1 linen in blue and 40/2 in white lace linen combine to give a white centre and coloured edges. 26 pairs

15 Staggered motifs given cohesion by outlining trails

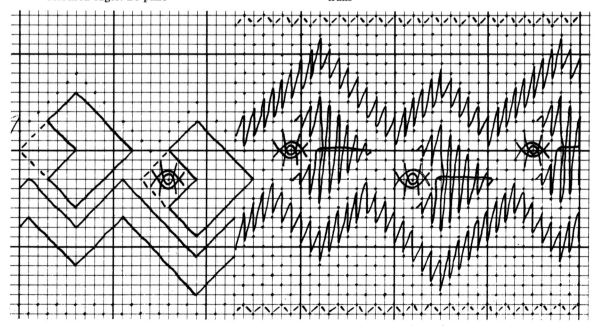

In . . . lace goods generally, a heavy mass of unbroken tone or colour is not satisfactory. The fabric is, in the first place, light in itself: you may have a bold design if you please, but it must have lightness; it should be varied in weight; the material depends for its effect upon light passing through it, therefore, give light its opportunity, and design in conjuction with this helpmate.[2]

∗ *Texture* is an important element of lace, but we can make a lot more of it by weaving in specially shiny, sparkly or knobbly threads.

Some other useful points to bear in mind are:

∗ Keep it simple. Too much detail, too many fancy stitches, too many colours, may destroy the impact. Go for a definite effect and subordinate your design to that. You may have several ideas on how to interpret a pattern – better three distinct designs than one mish-mash.

∗ Keep it narrow. Patterns will always end up wider than you imagine.

∗ Keep the repeats short. The corners will be easier and you will not lose your rhythm.

16 Bockens 16/1 linen in russet, with trails each in one thread of super spun silk 9G. 36 pairs

∗ The eye is most used to working from left to right, so it is useful to design patterns in that direction. But one usually works with the wrong side uppermost. Design and trace your pattern as you want it, and reverse the direction (turn the tracing over) when photocopying or pricking, if you wish to utilize this point. While on the subject of direction, it is worth making the point that artists also use upward rising elements to express life and vitality, and downwards drooping ones to express death and decay.

Let us now take a simple motif familiar to all Torchon workers – the heart, arrow-head or chevron – and work up some patterns, making use of some of the points already made. The *asymmetrical* aspect of this shape makes it a good one to emphasize *direction,* and it works easily from any angle (see fig. 10).

1) Let us point it first of all from left to right. This turns out to be so strong (fig. 11) that little else need be done with it; it is a good idea to hang it from a fair depth of simple ground, and add a simple edging which will not detract from the main emphasis of the pattern (fig. 12). (The edging here is very simple – the outer pin-holes

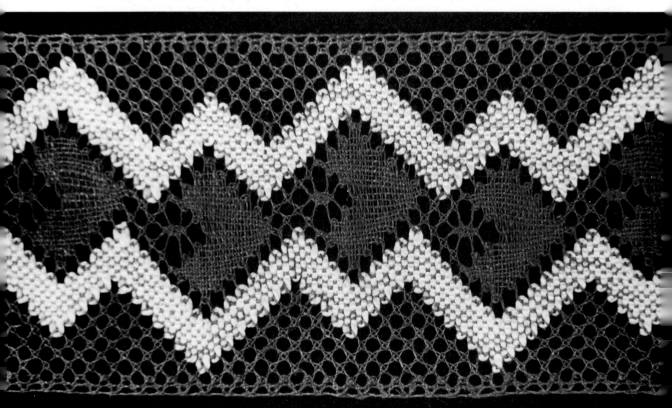

are drawn vertically beneath the inner ones to allow the impression of a series of points, instead of the usual scallops. See fig. 44 for a selection of useful edgings.)

2) We will now *reverse* the motif, and break up the *rhythm* by leaving a gap between each pair of motifs (fig. 13). Since the gap leaves a useful diamond-shaped hole between the chevrons, one could add *emphasis* by making this an eyelet. A simple scalloped trimming on both sides will allow this to be used with a threading of ribbon, but the uneven arrangement of the elements means an *irregular* edging – itself, no bad thing. It has been made up here with the four outer passives and the worker, in each edging, in a coloured thread, with a further pair used as one would a gimp, with plenty of twists, to outline each head, to give a coloured edge and white centre to the pattern (fig. 14).

3) Now face the motif back in one direction, but stagger it slightly (fig. 15). Even with the addition of a spider, the motifs are now too far away from each other, and a further element must be added to reintroduce *cohesion* – outlining trails, which can be made in a contrasting thread, make this a useful pattern both horizontally and vertically. Such an active pattern needs to be toned down with a straight edge, to make an insertion (fig. 16).

4) The motifs lock together quite well pointing up and down, but this does look boring. Further rows add interest, but now there is too much going on. If only alternate vertical groups are retained, these can be further emphasized in the making up, by being made in a contrasting colour; or they could be made in half-stitch to contrast with whole-stitch. A simple edging has been added, but again needs to be slightly irregular (figs 17 and 18).

5) The motifs can be compacted, and lend themselves well to being drawn up into a square mat

17 Motifs pointing up and down

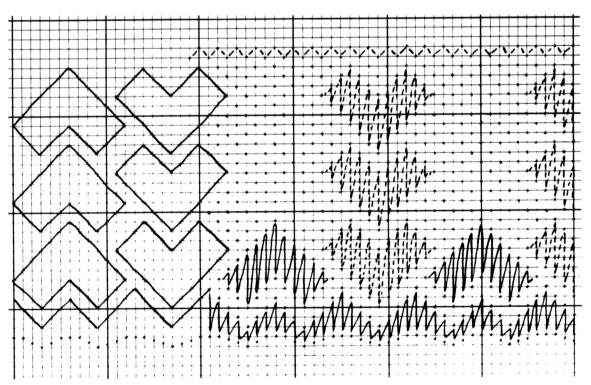

18 Russet linen used for the main body of passives, with blue introduced in the edge and in alternate rows of motifs. 33 pairs

(fig. 19). The edging is again irregular, and interest has been added to the centre with a patch of rose ground. The outer motifs were made with just one pair of contrast colour workers (fig. 20).

19 Square mat with rose ground centre

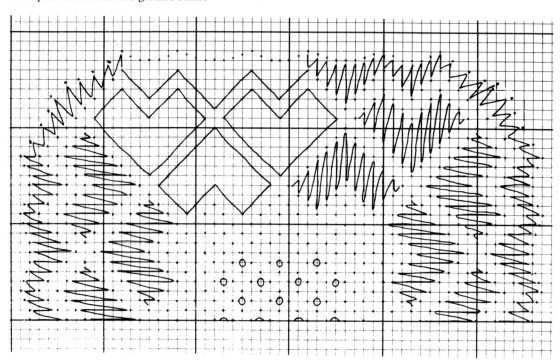

20 One contrasting pair of workers has been used
to make all the outer motifs (best seen on colour
plate 1). Blue and russet Bockens linen 16/1. 29
pairs

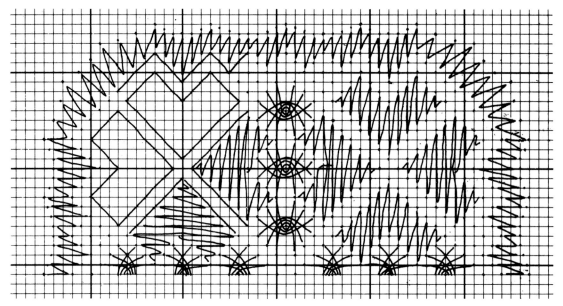

6) Moving on from there, the motifs make an ideal cluster, which can be grouped to form another mat (fig. 21). The space between each group of motifs is ideal for spiders. A simple, regular edging has been added to this busy pattern (fig. 22).

21 Cluster mat with spiders

22 Mat made up in Bockens linen 16/1, russet. 26 pairs

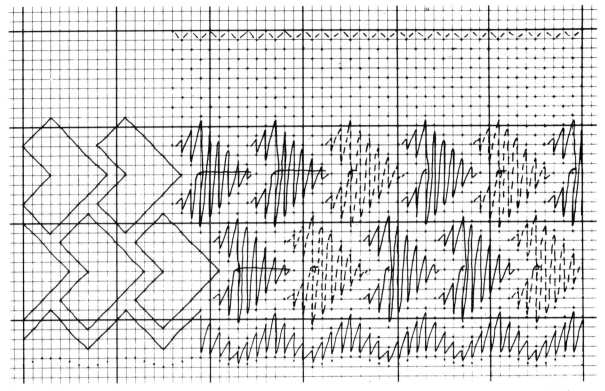

23 Double rows of motifs

24 Lace linen 40/2, alternate groups of half and whole stitch motifs. 38 pairs

7) Before we finish with the motif, let us look again at what can be done with a single direction, but double rows (fig. 23). Interest can be added by making the motifs in groups of half-stitch and whole-stitch, giving a subtly irregular appearance (fig. 24).

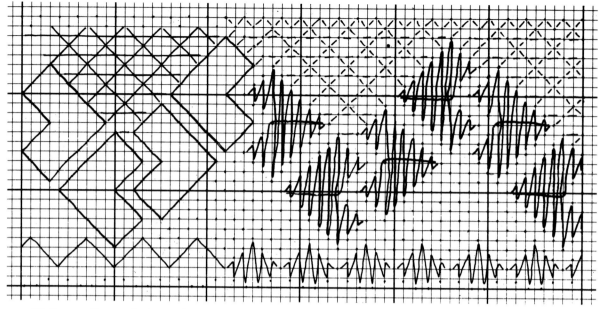

25 Jigsaw-effect, with the emphasis to the bottom

8) Finally, by locking the pieces together in jigsaw fashion, one can achieve an even more irregular appearance, although each repeat is still the same (fig. 25). The *emphasis* is placed to the bottom, by lightening the top ground space with honeycomb stitch. A small, totally regular edging draws it all together (fig. 26).

26 Made up in 16/1 linen, blue. 30 pairs

Colour plate 1 shows the results of this exercise, which was turned into an experiment in interpretation, using both widely-used lace threads and weaving thread. Weaving thread in two complementary colours and a thicker texture have been used to increase the range of possibilities, thereby giving you the chance to see and judge the value of using new threads.

There are many more ways of re-arranging this motif – see what you can do. Try mixing vertical and horizontal motifs; or deliberately design patterns with top, bottom, central, vertical or horizontal emphasis. Play with other motifs, too – the more you can extract from simple elements, the easier you will find it to handle those more complex.

A little learning is a dangerous thing! If and when you find pattern design becoming an absorbing occupation, and wish to know more, you may like to read some of the more technical books recommended at the end of this chapter. In them, you will discover that there are only seven kinds of border pattern; all known patterns can be shown to conform to these groups.

Taking our chevron (shaded to make it quite irregular), these seven borders would work out as in fig. 27. The technical terms of pattern making are *translation*, where the motif simply repeats without changing; *reflection*, where it repeats in mirror-image (horizontally or vertically); *rotation*, where it turns about a point; and *glide*, where it shifts diagonally out of the horizontal or vertical.

If you knew too soon that there are only seven pattern groups, you might only look for seven, whereas in fact there are many variations you can derive from each group.

Booklist

Pattern Design, Lewis F. Day, Batsford, 1933 (but still in print).

Pattern: its structure and geometry, Richard Padwick and Trevor Walker, Ceolfrith Press, 1977. Very good

Handbook of Regular Patterns, Peter S. Stevens, MIT Press, 1980. Expensive, but exhaustive

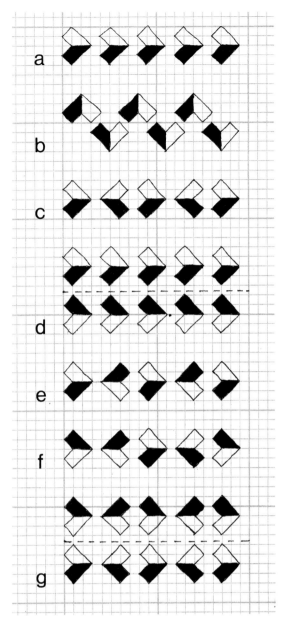

27 The seven basic border patterns: (a) translation; (b) translation of a glide reflection; (c) translated reflection; (d) reflected translation; (e) rotation, translation; (f) reflection, glide reflection, rotation and translation; (g) two horizontal reflections, and vertical reflection

The Sense of Order, E.H. Gombrich, Phaidon, 1979. History

Pattern Design, Archibald H. Christie, Dover, 1969. History

Abstract Design, Amor Fenn, Batsford, 1930

5 | Compound patterns

So far, we have been making simple patterns from just one shape, but many patterns combine several different elements. These 'compound' patterns may appear complicated, yet even these have simple beginnings.

Let us take a simple shape and build upon it until we have something satisfying. Probably the most basic repeat element which fits in Torchon grid is the diamond. In this exercise we shall draw a very simple diamond shape, and repeat it so that it becomes just one element in a larger design. This was suggested by the way patchworkers take a simple 'block' and repeat it to produce an interesting new overall pattern.

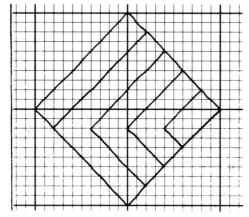

28 Basic diamond with some lines drawn inside

The basic diamond has been drawn over four adjacent inch squares on $\frac{1}{10}$in graph paper (fig. 28). Absolute beginners may find it confusing to draw patterns straight on to graph paper, but all you have to remember is that your Torchon grid uses adjacent diagonal intersections – i.e. each *alternate* vertical or horizontal intersection. You may prefer to use a dotted grid to start with (fig. 30). The same size of diamond would have 11

dots along each side, inclusive of the corner dots (fig. 29). Within that area, draw a number of diagonals along the lines of the grid. Keep it simple, and if one arrangement of lines does not yield some useful shapes, abandon it and try another – you may have to persevere before inspiration strikes!

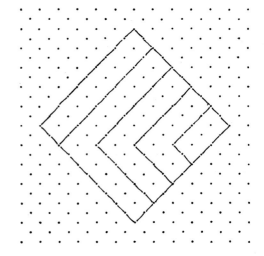

29 The same shape drawn on dotted grid

30 Dotted grid, drawn from $\frac{1}{10}$in graph paper

31 The basic shapes repeated by *translation* and *glide*, then shaded

The next stage is to play with the shape, repeating it by tracing over it, moving the tracing on and tracing again, until you have built up an area covered with pattern. You will see that in fig. 31 the shape is repeated (by 'translation' and 'glide') in the same direction, and emphasis is given by shading the alternate channels produced. In fig. 32, the shape has been mirrored or 'reflected' (by turning the tracing paper over), and then the intervening spaces have been filled

32 A better solution seems to be to *reflect* and *rotate* the shape

by mirroring the shape back-to-back, which 'rotates' it. As this is repeated, a more interesting pattern begins to emerge. In this case, note that a continuous border pattern has appeared at the centre. This sort of effect should be looked for so that it can be isolated and worked on further (fig. 33).

Torchon is easiest to make in simple shapes, so the alternating centre-spots are isolated and their elements simplified (fig. 34). This is too simple, so more variety is added by using thick and thin trails, and emphasizing alternate pattern areas – but this makes the unbroken motif too dominant (fig. 35). The final shape has aimed at evening-up

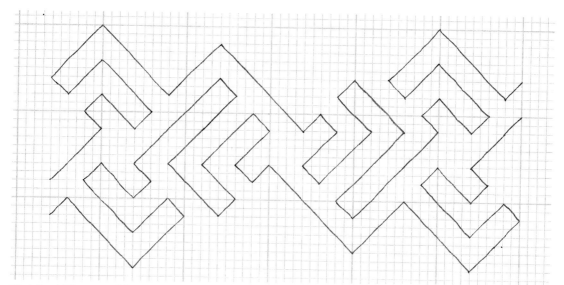

33 (*above*) The central feature is isolated

34 (*below*) Alternating centres are emphasized and simplified

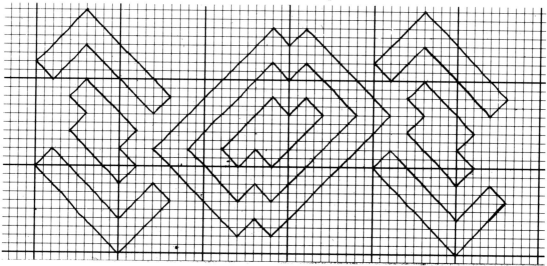

35 Variety is added

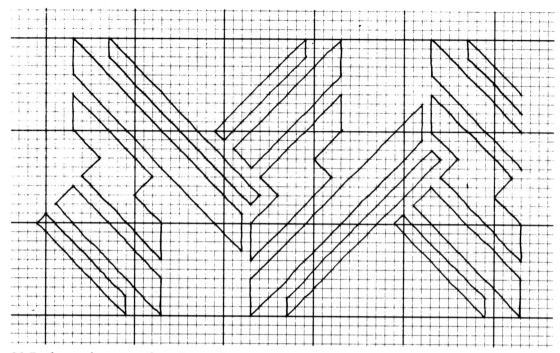

36 Further work evens up the pattern and
emphasizes the zig-zag motifs

the whole pattern and emphasizing the central
zig-zag shape (fig. 36).

The watchword here is patience. It may take
you several evenings, rubbing bits out of the
pattern, thinking about the alternatives, emphasizing other areas, until at last an interesting and
practical pattern emerges. One might be tempted
to stop at the first sign of a useful pattern, but it is
often worth carrying on to see if balance and
proportion can be improved. Success is very much
in the eye of the beholder – only you can tell when
a pattern satisfies you. In the example shown, the
pattern could be worked on further; for example
by abstracting the zig-zag motif and emphasizing
'lightning' shapes, or by widening the pattern so
that more shapes join up.

The patterns created for Torchon can also be
transferred to other media; for example, the
original shape from fig. 33 could make a good
quilting pattern. One of the most successful
British patchwork designers, Pauline Burbidge,
builds up her complex geometric patterns from
quite simple beginnings and experiments with
endless variations:

I try to select the strongest, most pleasing design. This
process is not always easy, but I always play by instinct
– if a design feels totally right, this means that the
labour that is to follow will be worth while. People often
say to me: 'What patience you have to sew all those bits
of fabric together!', but really I think the patience is
needed in the designing, to keep going until I am really
satisfied.

The pattern that resulted from the exercise in this
chapter (figs 37 and 38) needed a corner, and the
classic way of designing a corner is to stand a
pocket mirror on the diagonal of your pattern and
to run it along until a good shape emerges. What
is a 'good corner'? It ought to be one which does
not disrupt the flow of the pattern, one which
looks all of a piece with it. Additionally, if one
creates a mirrored corner, one may need a
mirrored 'turnover' to reverse the pattern half
way along the straight length of the pattern. The
turnover suggested here was created by placing a
mirror on the tail of one of the zig-zag motifs. It
overlaps with seven lines at the bottom of the
pattern.

37 The pattern that results, including a corner

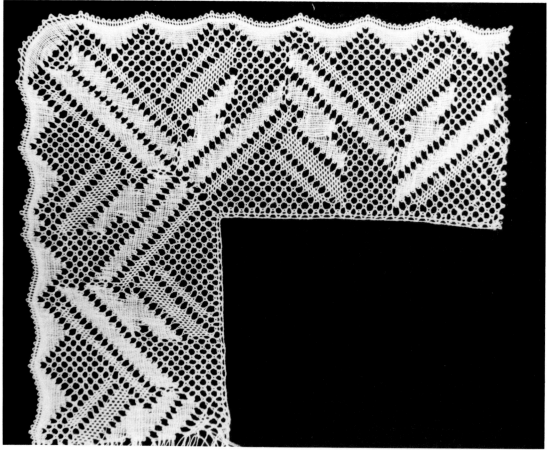

38 The $\frac{1}{10}$ in pattern has been reduced twice on the photocopier, and worked in 120 linen thread. 41 pairs

39 Campbells linen 70 was used by Betty Wilson to make up the pattern. 52 pairs

The shape in this chapter transfers quite easily on to circular grid (which will be dealt with more fully in Chapter Seven) and the pattern can be widened to allow some of the cut trails to join up (figs 39 and 40). Some lacemakers may prefer

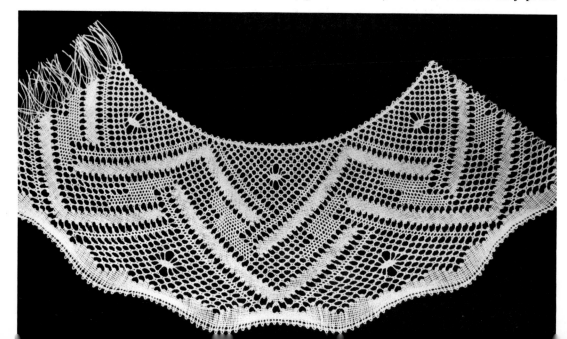

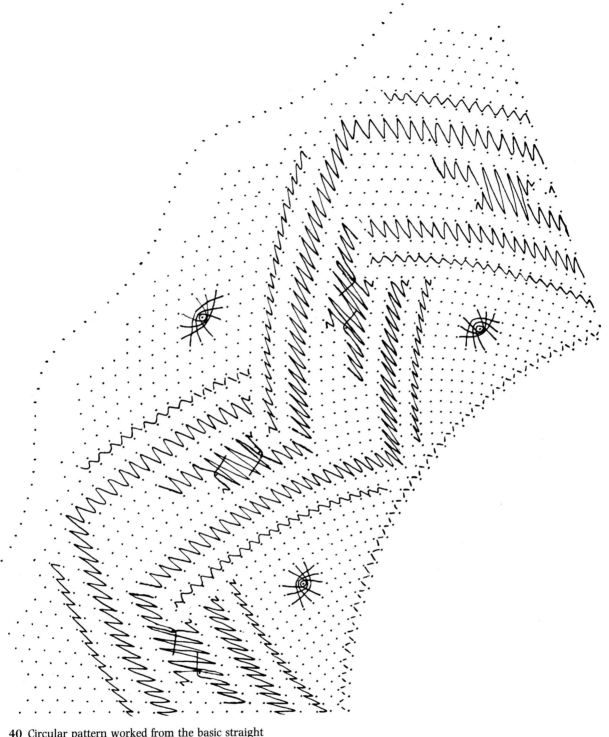

40 Circular pattern worked from the basic straight
one (nine repeats make a full circle, inside
diameter 8in (203mm), outside diameter 16½in
(419mm))

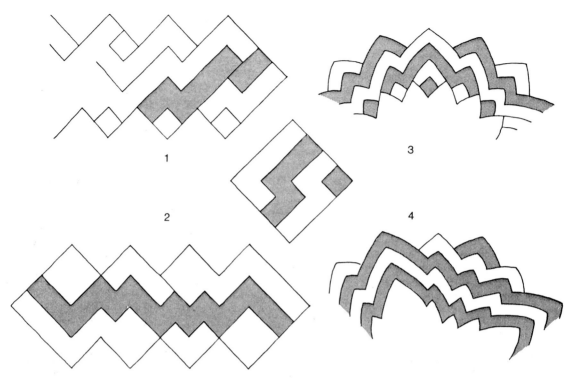

41 A similar system of work, with the features overlapping. A number of interesting ideas are emerging, but the fourth was the one used

straight edgings to be fairly narrow, because they know they will have to do many repeats, whereas with a circular pattern it is obvious that there will be a limited number of repeats, so the pattern could be wider and more elaborate.

The satisfying result of such an exercise is that the pattern owes nothing to anyone else – it is a purely personal creation. Unlike other design methods, this needs no outside inspiration and is really an organized 'doodle'. The system has been

used by Ann Dukes, who chose an even simpler first shape, and then overlapped it rather than repeating it exactly. An interesting irregular trail emerges (fig. 41). Ann wished to work directly on to polar grid, and found her ideas limited by the fact that you can only get a limited number of repeats on this grid (see Chapter Seven). She chose a five-repeat shape, and by skilful use of stitches, created a design which has an almost 3D effect. She then went back and explored other possibilities – producing the basis for a highly effective and original table setting from the simplest of beginnings (fig. 42).

42a Three mats worked from the original idea, with different numbers of repeats. Designed and worked by Ann Dukes

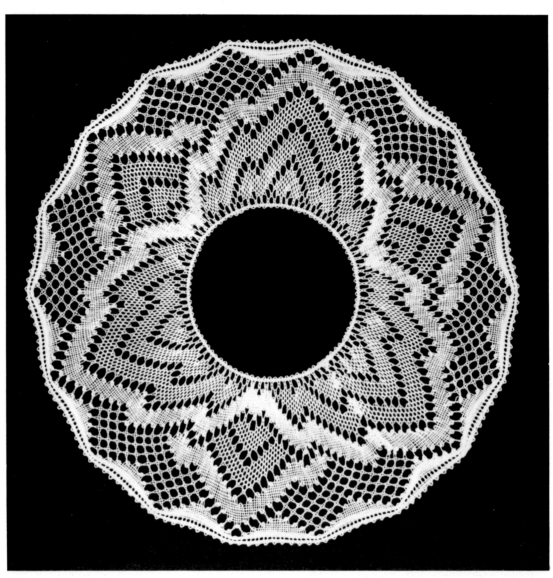

42b

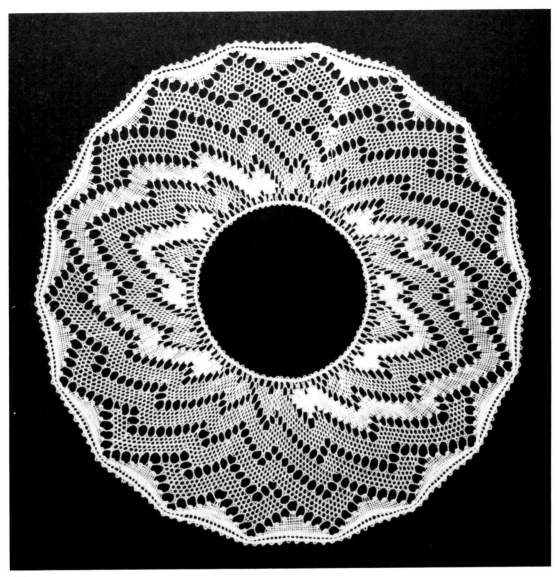

42c

6 | Lavender bag

When learning a new technique, it often helps to be given a specific, easy project to do. The only way to test whether you have designed a viable lace pattern is to make it up, so I suggest you try a small lavender bag edging, which will be quick both to design and to make, and can be put to use either at home or as a gift.

There are several approaches you can take to pattern design. You might see an inspiring motif, try it out on graph paper to see how it would work in lace, and then decide in what kind of pattern you wish to incorporate it. You may design with a specific use in mind, but not be too concerned about the size of the eventual pattern. Or you may be set, or set yourself, definite limits within which your pattern must be confined. Surprising though it may sound, the latter approach is often the easiest. Archibald H. Christie wrote in *Pattern Design*:

In exploring the unknown possibilities of a definite proposition, it will be found that ideas flow, one from another, with a readiness that unguided effort could never attain; for it cannot be repeated too insistently, that definite restrictions in no wise trammel composition, but are actually an incentive to more intense concentration.

For this exercise, I describe how to work around a 2in centre hole for the sachet, but some students may wish to rub that hole out in the end and make a square mat; others may decide they wish to turn one side into a yard-lace pattern. The purpose of the exercise is just to get you started on some practical pattern planning. Absolute beginners may find it less confusing to work on the grid in fig. 30, or you may prefer, as I do, to work straight on to graph paper.

Draw the 2in centre square in the middle of

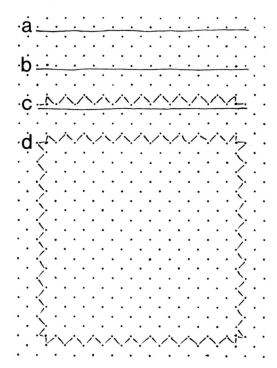

43 Planning the centre hole for the lavender bag edging, on dotted grid

44 A selection of simple Torchon edgings:
(a), (d) fans with two different ways of treating the centre; (b), (c) simple fan with two types of corners; (e), (f) a dipped head can be drawn up in a similar way to a raised head; (g), (h) the inner and outer edges can be more complicated; (i) feather; (j) very simple edge, with corner; (k) large fan with spider; (l) French fan; (m), (n) scallops; (o) German spider. The basic difference between (e), (f) and (g), (h), (j) is the position if the outer dot – directly above the inner dot (e), (f) or half-way between (g), (h), (j). The former gives a pointed edging, the latter a rounded one

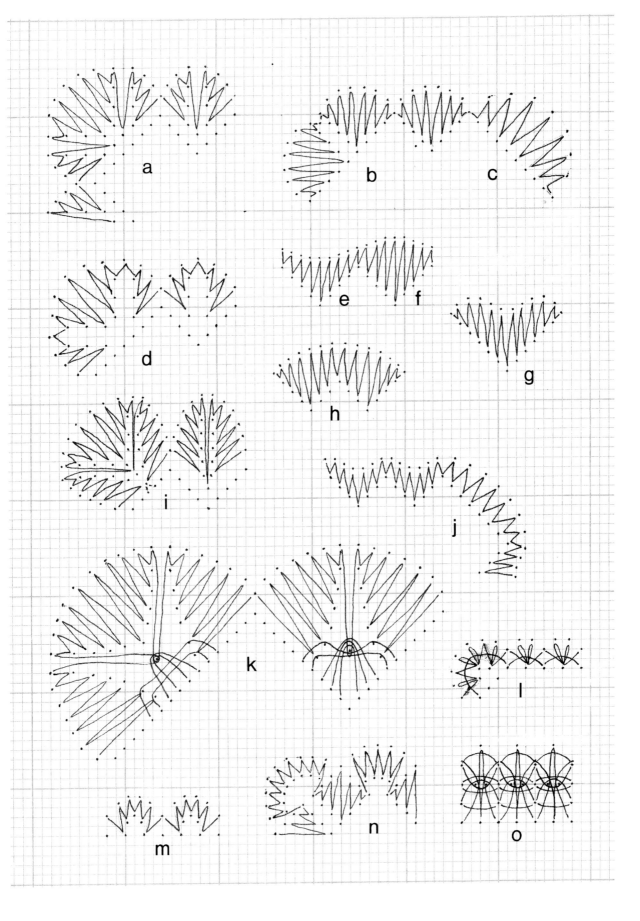

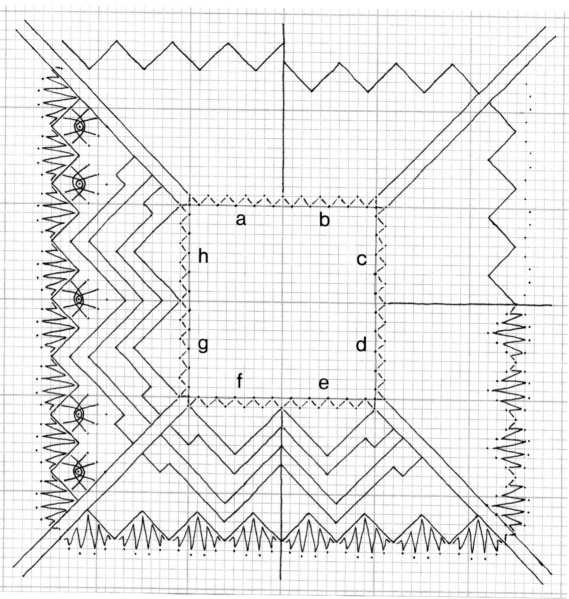

45 Basic steps to a first edging

your page, which if you are using the dotted grid (fig. 43) means:

a) Underline 12 horizontal dots, to mark out the basis of your foot.

b) Put an extra dot between the first two and the last two – these are the corner dots.

c) Join these dots with those in the line above with a zig-zag line, to show the foot.

d) Repeat that around three more sides – remember that each new line overlaps at the corner dot.

Then measure it! Make sure you have not gone wrong – it should measure 2in between the corner dots. Choose a different size if you prefer, but it is essential to ensure each side is the same length.

Now you should draw up a framework of guidelines so that you know exactly where to work:

∗ Draw in the lines which show where you will turn the corners.

∗ Add a line in the centre of each side – now all you have to do for a symmetrical edging is design half of one side and repeat that seven times for the completed design.

∗ Mark in an edging.

Fig. 44 shows a page of edgings drawn on graph paper so that they are easy to transfer to your own patterns. Choosing one of the simplest, and electing to have four dots along each side of the fan, we need to mark in the edging so that it repeats evenly round the pattern. Using an even number of heads each side, we will just try drawing it out (fig. 45):

a) It misses by one dot.

b) So bring it down one dot.

c) Mark in the dots at the outer edge of the pattern.

d) Mark in the direction of your edge workers.

e, f) Draw in a simple pattern shape – this one has been taken from a computer board shown in a magazine advertisement (fig. 46).

g, h) Think how to fill the spaces left between the pattern and the edging – here we will add some simple spiders.

46 The printed circuit board shown in a magazine advertisement for a television suggested the motif used in the previous figure

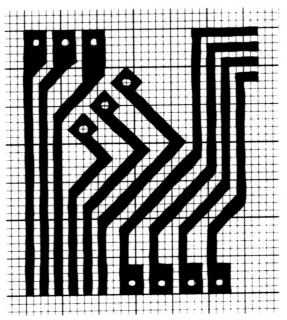

47 The completed pattern, traced and copied

The completed pattern (figs 47 and 48) has been made up with the trails in two shades of lavender and the rest of the lace in white; but in one colour the trails could be in half and whole stitch. We have created a pattern with a definite all-over effect, mirrored at centres and corners.

Let us look at different effects you could get within a similar framework – although the edge has been taken further out to give a little more room to play with – by adding one extra head; nine instead of eight.

If you look at fig. 49, side (a) has been designed with shapes that draw the eye inward; side (b) with shapes pointing outwards; side (c) has overlapping trails; and (d) is for those who prefer a 'stop' pattern which is not quite so bold; but diamonds of whole or half stitch towards the centre would add textural interest. Two types of edging, pointed or rounded, with corners have been added, so that any of these shapes may be traced off as patterns.

48 The pattern made up, in nett silk 50 and two lavender shades of embroidery silk. 20 pairs

49 Different effects which can draw the eye in, take it out, offer overlapping trails, or use simple spiders and diamonds

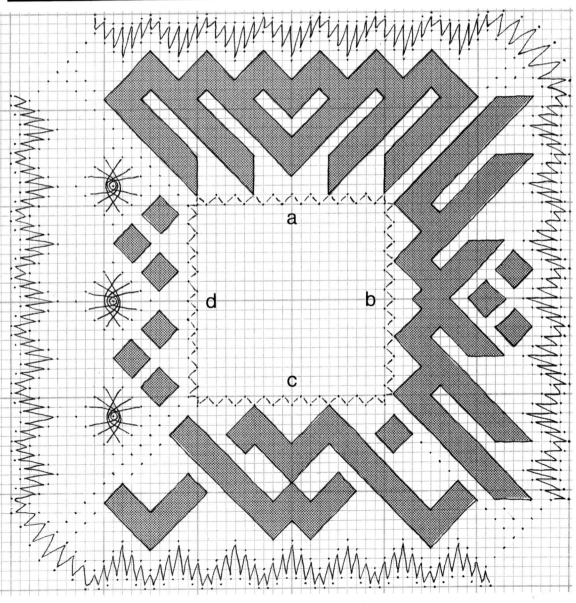

a

b

c

d

50 (*above*) Finer pattern with overlapping trails

51 (*below*) Pattern made up in 300/4 silk, with one corner emphasized in whole-stitch. 24 pairs

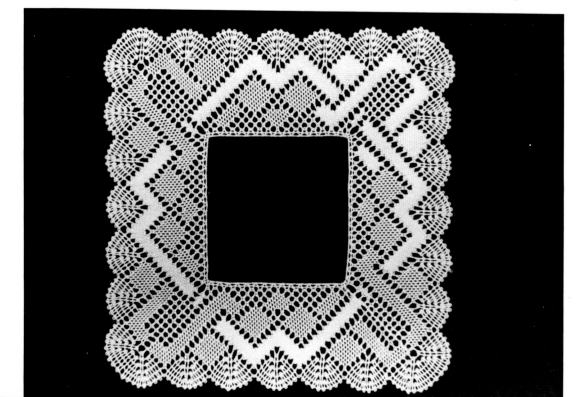

Another example of a pattern with overlapping trails (fig. 51) has the 'M' shape a little more pronounced, and special attention paid to the corners. It was designed on a finer grid taken from Pamela Nottingham's *The Technique of Torchon Lace*. One of the first I did, it was an elaboration of a simpler, coarser pattern, and is shown here because it became a useful step on the way to further refinement.

It made quite a pretty pattern, but much work could still be done on it. The final chapter in this book takes this initial, imperfect idea and attempts to demonstrate that if you continue to play with a pattern you can reach far more satisfying conclusions.

Do not forget when drafting blocks of cloth-stitch to leave channels between adjacent blocks (if you do not wish them to join) or between a block and an edging. This may seem obvious, but it is something people tend to forget at first.

Try to draw your shapes boldly. I draw the outlines of pattern elements along the intersections of the graph paper, and only draw in the pattern markings (most of the dots and the direction of the worker threads, etc.) when I make the final tracing. This makes the initial pattern draft very easy to follow.

Try to go for a definite effect, casting your net of light and shade with real purpose in mind. You can:

* Draw the eye in to the centre.

* Send it out to each edge.

* Emphasize the corners.

* Emphasize just one corner.

* Send the eye round the pattern in a clockwise or anti-clockwise direction (with an asymmetrical pattern).

* Emphasize the symmetry of the centre of each side.

* Make each side different.

* Emphasize the edging, with a very quiet supporting pattern.

You can gain extremely useful experience by trying out different ideas, just for the fun of it. Pattern practice is often just a question of loosening up the mind. Set yourself problems to solve, and then draw, erase, draw, change – until something interesting starts to emerge. Perhaps you may feel you cannot start because you have no end results in mind? Excellent! Something *will* appear once you set pencil to paper. You may not know what pattern may appear from one day's end to the next, but experience has shown that something always does emerge to reward your efforts.

7 | Different grids

Up to this point, we have been working on square graph paper, producing rigid patterns. Things can get very interesting, however, if you learn how to use different grids which will allow your pattern shapes to bend and flow. You will find that graph paper is also available in full circles, quarter segments, logarithm cycles, perspective shapes, rectangles (known as hypometric) and

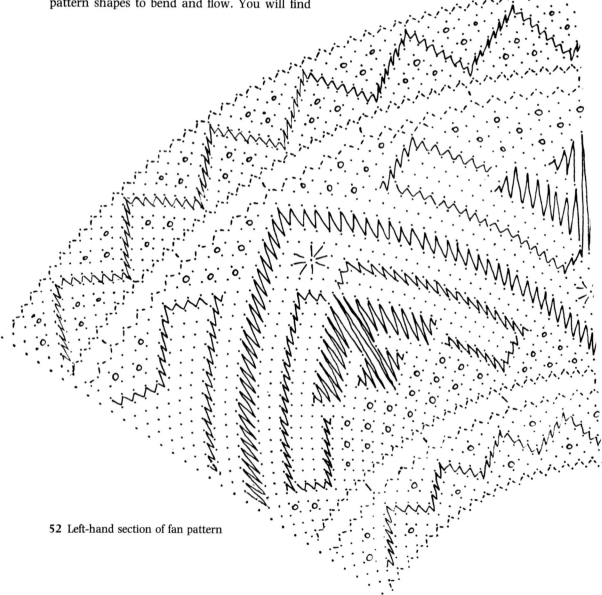

52 Left-hand section of fan pattern

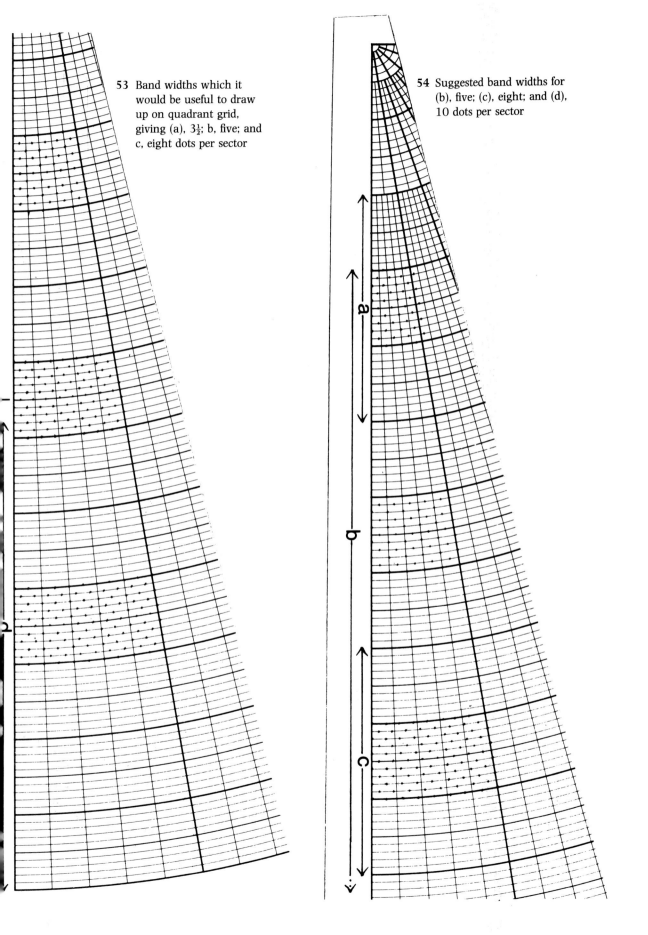

53 Band widths which it would be useful to draw up on quadrant grid, giving (a), 3½; b, five; and c, eight dots per sector

54 Suggested band widths for (b), five; (c), eight; and (d), 10 dots per sector

hexagons (isometric) – or you can make up new ones.

If you want to use a graph paper for Torchon lace, you first have to establish a grid of suitable dots. There is no alternative to the tedium of drawing in each dot individually, which may take many hours on a large polar or quadrant grid. But once it is completed, you will have an invaluable tool with a lifetime's use. Let us look at some of the most useful ones.

Quadrants

This is one of the most useful grids, a quarter segment, sold by Chartwell in pads and by good lace suppliers in single sheets. There are many different grids you can make, for different purposes such as fans, collars of all sizes, circular mats, and ruffles (a straight edging transferred on to a curved grid will ruffle beautifully when used straight). However, unlike square graph paper, where the dots are always the same distance apart, here the sectors change vastly in width as they move away from the centre. You must either work over an area small enough so that one thread thickness can still accommodate the variations, or split your pattern into bands, varying the dot pitch so that each sector contains dots at a fairly even distance apart over the whole width of the pattern.

You can vary the dot pitch to accommodate different thicknesses of thread. The pitches used here are for a medium fine thread like *fil à dentelles*, 100 cordonnet, 300/4 silk; and 80 Swedish linen.

It is a good idea to be flexible about where to change the dot pitch – you may need to change at the best place for a particular pattern, which may suit no other pattern. It is suggested you keep several grids with broad bands of dots plotted on them, so you can interchange as and when necessary.

From the centre outwards, it would be useful to draw dots at:

* Three-and-a-half dots per sector (fig. 52a).

* Five dots per sector (fig. 52b, 53b).

* Eight dots per sector (fig. 52c, 53c).

* Ten dots per sector (fig. 53d).

Let us take, for example, the problems involved in drafting a fan pattern. Sets of fan sticks come in different sizes – the fan pattern given here has been drafted to fit the cheapest, and most easily obtainable, plastic sticks.

One way of tackling a fan design would be to join two sheets of quadrant graph paper to make a semi-circle. Lay your sticks on top, decide where to plot your pattern, and then draw up a grid – with suitable changes in dot pitch – to fit it. However, that grid could fit no other sticks. It may seem tedious, but if you draw up bands of dots as suggested in figs 52 and 53 on pairs of graph sheets, giving one broad sector of five dots per segment for the main body of the fan, and bands of three-and-a-half and eight dots per segment for the inner and outer edges, you then have grids to fit an infinite variety of fan sizes, and grids for mats and collars too.

You may choose not to split your fan pattern, or you may decide to have only one break instead of two. Look at old fans and see how the designers set them out. They often had a centre motif and two side panels, or a continuous design which still drew definite emphasis to the centre or one side. Three or five bold motifs may be preferable to a continuous band of smaller ones with no particular emphasis.

Draw the outline of your fan on a sheet of tracing paper and place it over the main body of your grid to decide where you wish to arrange your pattern shapes – and where to break the pattern. When the centre has been worked out, move the tracing to the grid with the inner and outer dots. Complete the edgings, deciding at the same time how you wish to join the different bands together.

Having drawn up your fan, you need to provide neat ends. A parallel line of alternately spaced dots will give a sturdy, cloth-stitch edge. (You may also find that the dots in the different bands do not all end at exactly the same place – the last couple of lines of centre dots may need to be stretched slightly to fit.) Note the addition of dots at the inner edge of the fan pattern (figs 54 to 58)

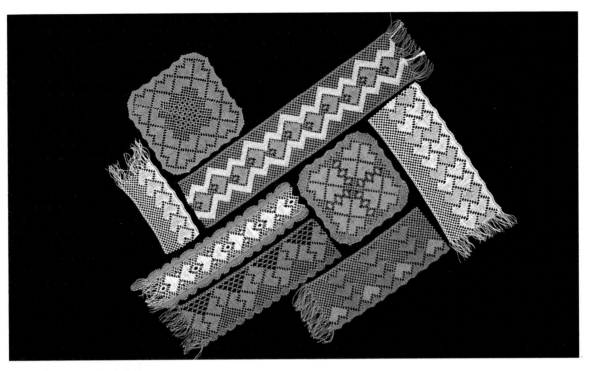

1 The simple pattern exercise from Chapter Four has been used to experiment with some of the threads suitable for $^1/_{10}$ in patterns. Plain patterns may be considerably enlivened by mixing colours and textures

2 Two shades of 300/4 Piper silk in lavender and purple, with extra threads of silver, make up the fan pattern

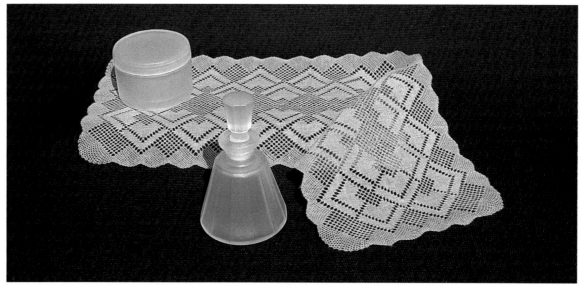

3 Pink linen was chosen for the dressing table runner, to match the make-up pots and the general decor of the room

4 Two different solutions for two lacemakers who wished to make up patterns in colour. **Coton perlé** was chosen for the red mat, and dyed with cold water dye; **fil à dentelles** was used for the pink mat, with just the worker pair at the edge and the outer passive in salmon pink. (Worked by Lin Allen and Betty Wilson)

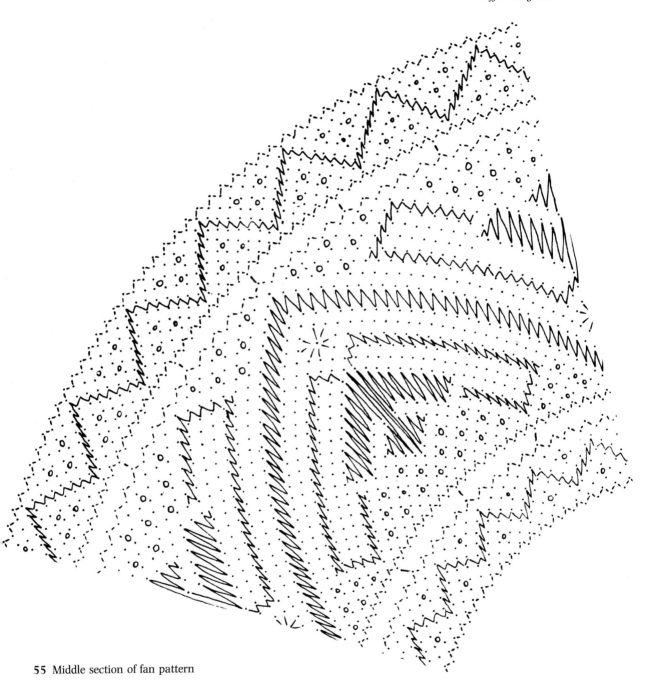

55 Middle section of fan pattern

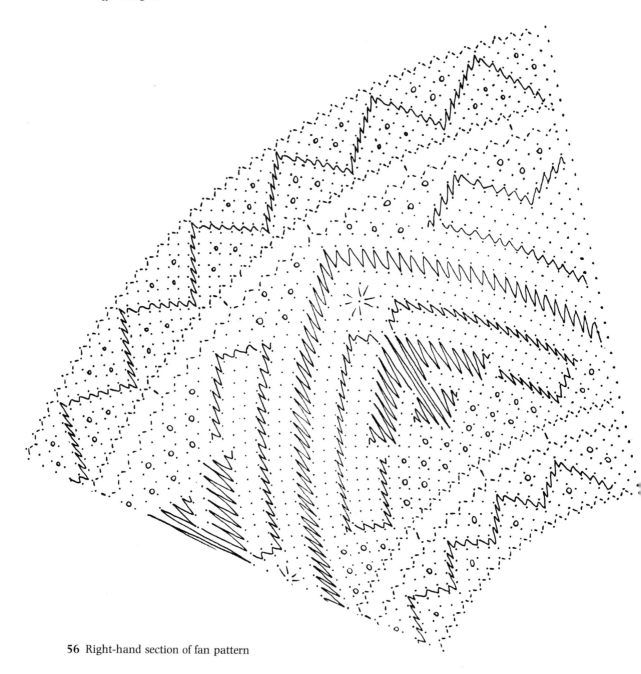

56 Right-hand section of fan pattern

to allow the addition of extra pairs to make a good foot at the edges of each band. Different fan designs will probably call for different treatment.

The motif for the fan pattern was inspired by the wrought-iron balcony of the library in the ornate Abbey of Melk glimpsed in a *Vogue* feature on Austria – you never know where a suitable motif will crop up. Hang in the pairs along the right-hand inner edge, work each band separately, joining each one to the next as you make the succeeding sectors, and then work the pairs into the trail along the left-hand edge, hanging them out from the centre of the trail as you go. Take care not to cut them off until well secured.

This is a simplistic approach to fan design – for a more technical approach, and help on folding, consult *Designing and Mounting Lace Fans* by Christine Springett. Adapting fan patterns to fit your own sticks is merely a question of re-drawing the existing pattern using the method outlined above. This can be a good introduction to fan design – you will probably find it much easier than you think.

I have not included a dress collar. One designed to fit me could so easily not fit you. Design your own – decide the size you want for the neck edge, then stand your tape measure upright along your grid (you will need three, or possibly four, quadrant segments joined together here) so you can determine exactly where your inner edge must be drawn. Only you know if you wish for a front or back opening, or a two-section Peter Pan shape. Instructions for beautifully designed collars are given by Pamela Nottingham and Jenny Fisher.

The outer section of 10 dots per segment is useful for large circular cloth edgings, or a bertha collar (see Chapter 10). You will need only one 90° segment of dots, since you are unlikely to want a pricking much bigger. To frill nicely, a bertha collar needs to be about one-and-one-fifth of a circle – for a pattern with three repeats per 90° segment, that would cover 14 repeats.

The bertha pattern (figs 62 and 63) is worked from an idea culled from a wallpaper pattern. This appeared to be made up of small pattern elements arranged in herringbone fashion (fig. 59). Sectors were first shaded in to give a curved pattern, and graded areas were then added either side to give lighter shades (fig. 60). The main pattern shape is done in whole stitch with lighter areas progressively in triangular ground, rose ground, half-stitch Torchon ground, and honeycomb. A more definite pattern shape could easily get lost in the folds of a bertha, whereas a softer shape like this could work much better. Twelve repeats make a full circle.

57 Completed fan leaf, worked in two shades of
300/4 silk with extra threads of DMC *fil d'argent*
to outline the main trail (see also colour plate
2). 74 pairs

58 Detail of central section of fan

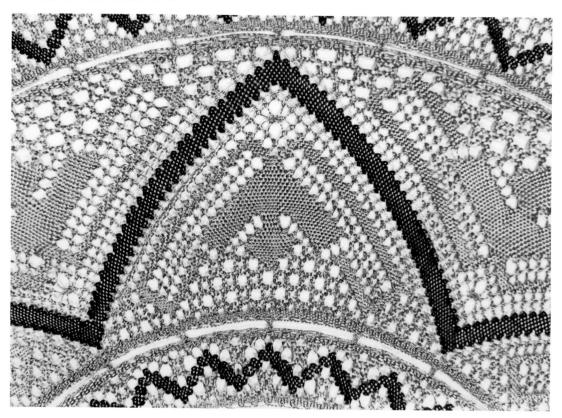

59 Herringbone shapes arranged on a 10 dots-per-sector quadrant grid

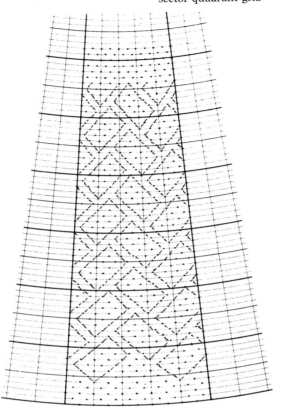

60 Different stitch densities gauged to arrange a gentle pattern

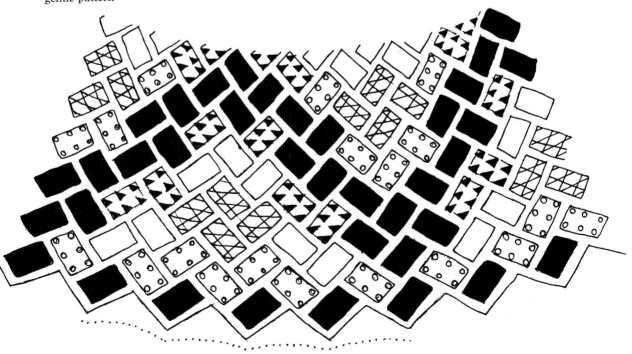

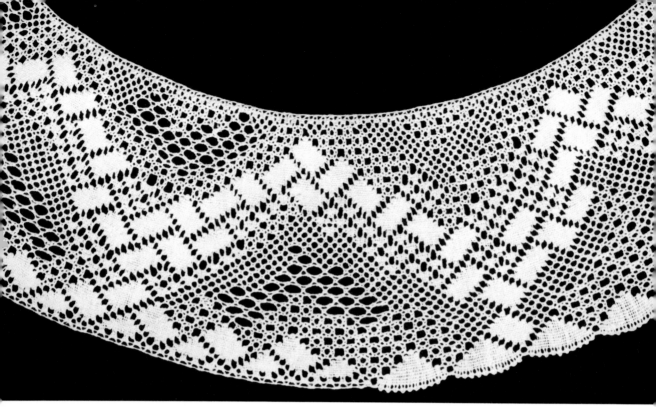

61 Several attempts were needed to arrange the
shapes harmoniously – the first (on the right)
was designed to be slightly irregular, but this
proved both irritating and lacking in contrast;
the second attempt was an improvement,
but it was still difficult to find the right edging
(40/2 linen)

62 A further re-arrangement of the motifs gives a
more harmonious effect. Try 70 or 80 linen for
household use; 300/4 or spun silk for dress use.
Made by Alison Fenny. 60 pairs

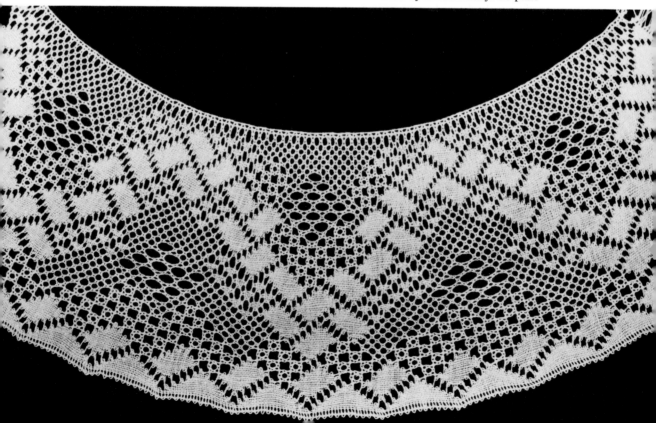

63 Pattern for final edging

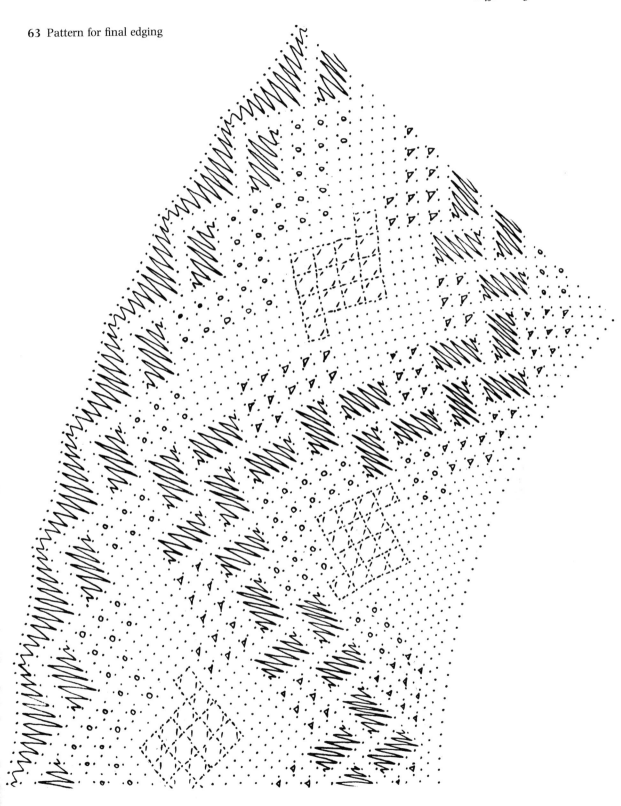

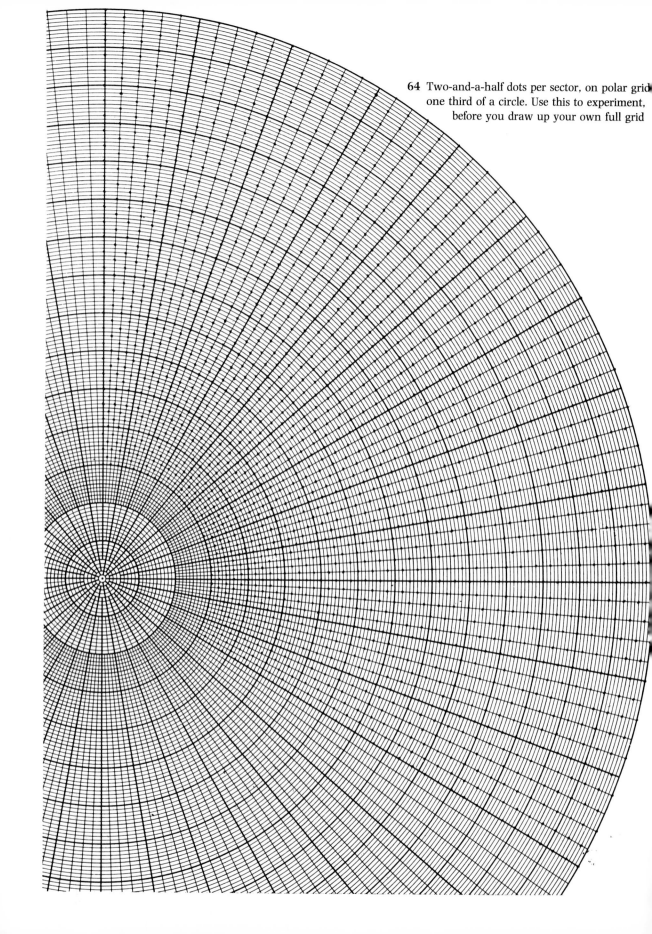

64 Two-and-a-half dots per sector, on polar grid one third of a circle. Use this to experiment, before you draw up your own full grid

65 Necklace pattern – left-hand side, plus
half of middle including central back-stitch

Full circles

Circular grids are also made in 360° polar sheets. One set of dots at 2½ dots per segment will be enough to see you through a variety of patterns from fine ones at the centre to quite coarse ones at the edge (fig. 64). The dots near the centre are already very close together, however, and it would not seem advisable to proceed much further in. There are 90 dots around the circumference of this grid, so the number of dots across the width of each pattern repeat must divide evenly into that total. A limited number of repeats prove viable: two (over 45 dots); three (over 30 dots); five (over 18 dots); six (over 15 dots); nine (over 10 dots); and 10 (over nine dots) are about the limit. You may find it necessary to modify designs to fit one of these, although a finer dot pitch would allow greater flexibility.

The outer section of this grid is just large enough for simple collars. The necklace collar shown in figs 65 to 67 originated from an Art Deco motif (fig. 68), and the shape was suggested by old Egyptian pharaonic jewelled collars. A

66 Necklace worked in Bockens Bomullsgarn cotton 16/2, and DMC *fil d'or* – two strands per bobbin if using the 'semi-fine' thread. Approx. 37 pairs

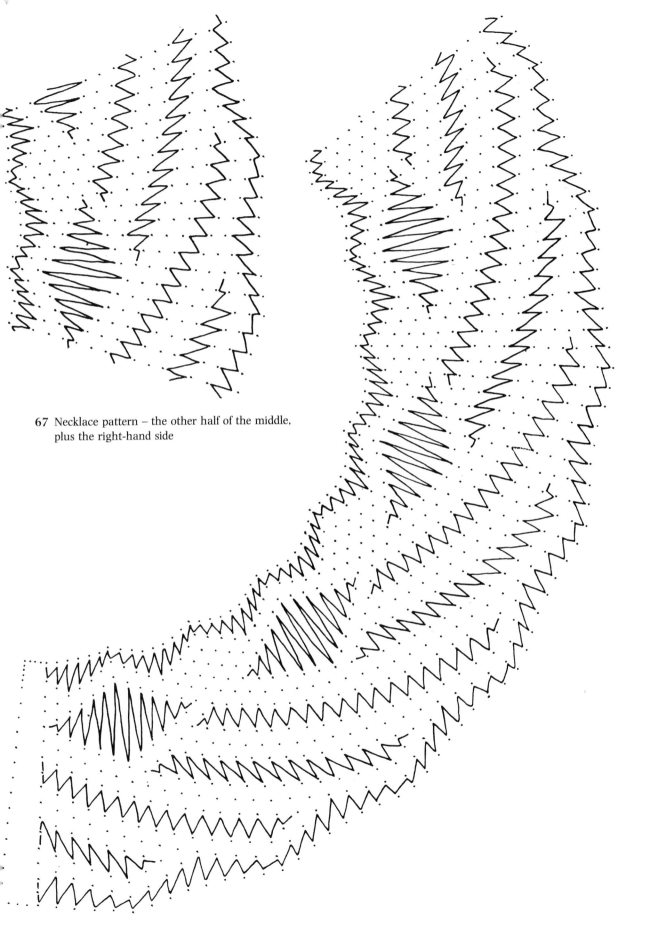

67 Necklace pattern – the other half of the middle, plus the right-hand side

68 Original Art Deco motif from *Art Deco Designs and Motifs* by Marcia Loeb

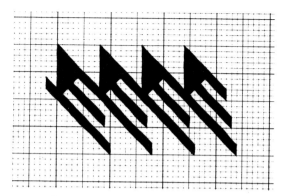

69 Motif turned into a border pattern

border pattern was first drawn up (fig. 69) and then simplified to facilitate working (fig. 70). The trails coming from the diamond motif have been worked in different directions and in half and whole-stitch to differentiate the densities (reversing at the centre), and the inner edge matches the outer edge – a straight foot was not found to be flattering at the neckline. The beginning and ending should be worked in a similar manner to the fan edge.

70 Border pattern simplified for application in collar design

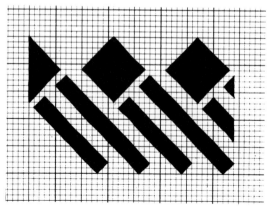

Irregular grids

Sometimes, events can set you off on a track that you might otherwise not have explored. Logarithmic grids looked at first sight to be too complicated

71 Section of Chartwell log graph sheet, four cycles, in millimetres and centimetres

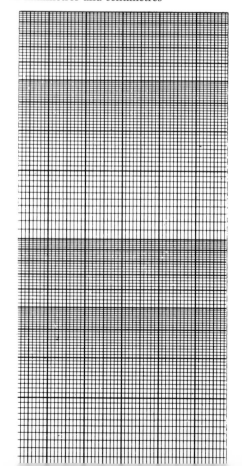

72 First section of dots traced from log graph sheet

73 One band of the log dots, isolated and repeated in mirror fashion to create a smooth flow of dense and widely-spaced dots

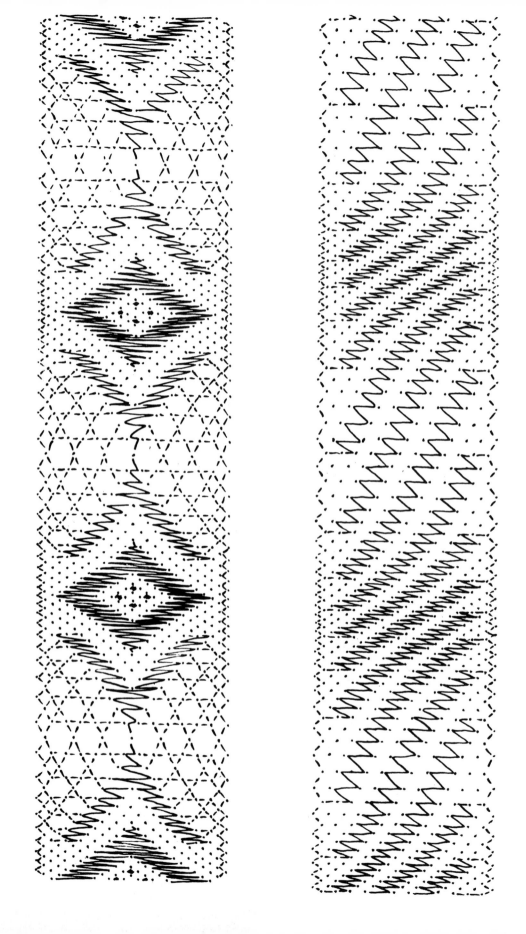

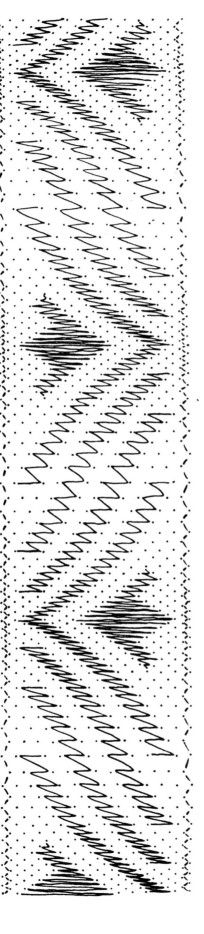

for lace, but the gift of one (fig. 71) prompted me to take a closer look. A grid was drawn up and the result certainly appeared interesting (fig. 72). Since log cycles contain wide variations, one area was isolated, grading evenly from close to wide dots. This was then mirrored to produce a grid (fig. 73), which offers curved trails in a straight pattern: this is quite an unusual feature for Torchon.

Motifs were drawn specifically to emphasize different aspects of the grid (figs 74 to 79), and sometimes only small sections of dots were used

74 Pattern emphasizing dense and open areas

75 Pattern to emphasize the curves that can be obtained with a graded grid

76 Arrowhead pattern

77 Dense and open lace, made in 300/4 silk, with a gold cord in the foot to increase stability. 28 pairs and foot cords

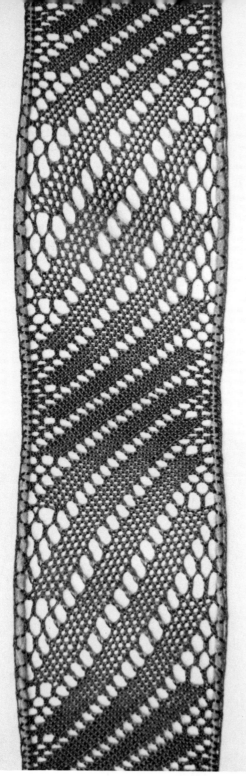

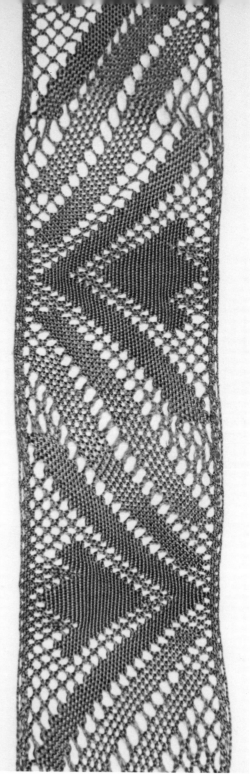

78 Curved pattern made up in blue 300/4 silk, with a thick silk thread in the foot. The trails can be thickened by changing the direction of the worker. 27 pairs

79 Arrowhead pattern made up in grey 300/4 silk – an experimental piece which led to fig. 76 being a slightly modified version. 30 pairs

and repeated. The resultant patterns lose in stability what they gain in interest, for different dot pitches give differing tensions to the lace. A coarse thread in the foot will add body (fig. 77 uses a gold cord), and all need to be mounted or inserted.

Hand-Drawn grids

In another case, an inquiry from a friend prompted me to investigate hand-drawn grids. An offer of assistance with drawing some grids was accepted with alacrity, and thought then had to be given to grids which would prove most useful. Since commercial laces with curved edges make very pretty trimmings for lingerie, this aspect was highlighted.

A wavy pattern section (fig. 80) was drawn with the aid of a French curve (obtainable from stationers). It depicts only a small section, in quite a large scale, but it was traced and repeated vertically, mirrored, and the resultant grid was reduced on the photocopier (fig. 81).

80 Grid made up from curved section, and reduced on photocopier

81 Wavy pattern section drawn on 1mm graph paper using a French curve, by Bill Raymond

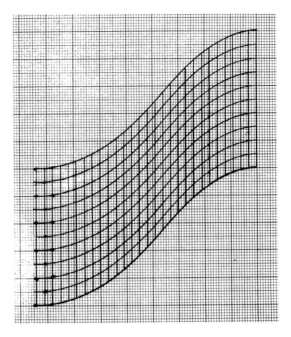

82 Wavy pattern, which aimed to make use of the flower shapes suggested by the curve of the dots

The resulting wavy pattern (fig. 82) was drafted to make the most of the interesting shapes offered by the lines of dots. Narrow laces making use of simple trails would appear to offer effective alternatives.

Other grids

We have been looking at easily available mathematical grids, but maths offers many other fruitful areas of study. Arabic 'Magic Squares' and the pleasing proportions offered by the Golden Section or Fibonacci Series have been used to

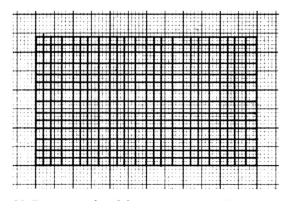

83 Experimental grid drawn on 1mm graph paper

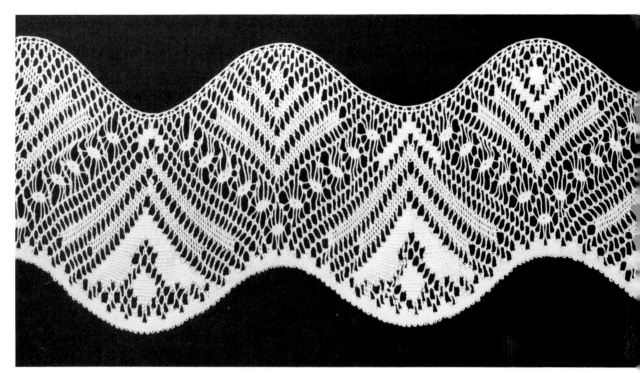

84 Resultant lace, made up in 300/4 silk. 34 pairs

great effect by designers in the past. Further investigation may be made in *Islamic Patterns* by Keith Critchlow, Thames and Hudson, 1976 (reprinted 1983).

Many other ideas can be investigated: dots may, for instance, be spaced on what could be called 'tartan' lines (fig. 83). Other variations could be tried on 1mm graph paper. Grids could even be drawn freehand to accommodate odd shapes. For those who have one, the home computer is also a potent source of interesting grids and design ideas.

8 | Outside inspiration

We have now looked at many different types of pattern: straight edgings, corners, squares, circular and irregular patterns. In several cases, patterns have been inspired by something seen in a book or magazine. Let us look more closely at that aspect, for it is one of the easiest ways of finding good shapes to put in your patterns.

You may be happier if you know the motif you use is entirely original to you, but successive generations of designers have always borrowed or copied from the past. In the search for pleasing patterns a good motif is all-important, since 'no beauty of detail will atone for an evil shape'.[1]

In this chapter, we will consider how to develop patterns inspired by a variety of sources.

Design source books

This is the easiest place to find new patterns. Here are several which will be particularly useful:

Japanese Border Designs, Theodore Menten, Dover, 1975

Pattern and Design with Dynamic Symmetry, Edward B. Edward, Dover, 1967

Art Deco Designs and Motifs, Marcia Loeb, Dover, 1972

Geometric Design and Ornament, Edmund V. Gillon Jr, Dover, 1969

Decorative Frames and Borders, Edmund V. Gillon Jr, Dover, 1973

A number of interesting motifs which looked suitable for Torchon have been taken from books such as these and drawn up as patterns:

1) *Japanese*

A shape from *Japanese Border Designs* (fig. 85) prompts conjecture. Is it a white shape on a black background, or a black shape on a white background? To see the different effects which can

85 Thought-provoking Japanese border pattern

stem from such a question, two prickings have been drawn from the one pattern, with the trail in the black pattern left as ground in the white pattern. Since the pattern itself is the important thing, the edge has been kept very simple (figs 86 to 89).

86 Interpretation as white on black (DMC *coton perlé* 12). 30/31 pairs

87 Interpretation as black on white (Bockens
Bomullsgarn 16/2). 30/31 pairs

88 Pattern for fig. 86

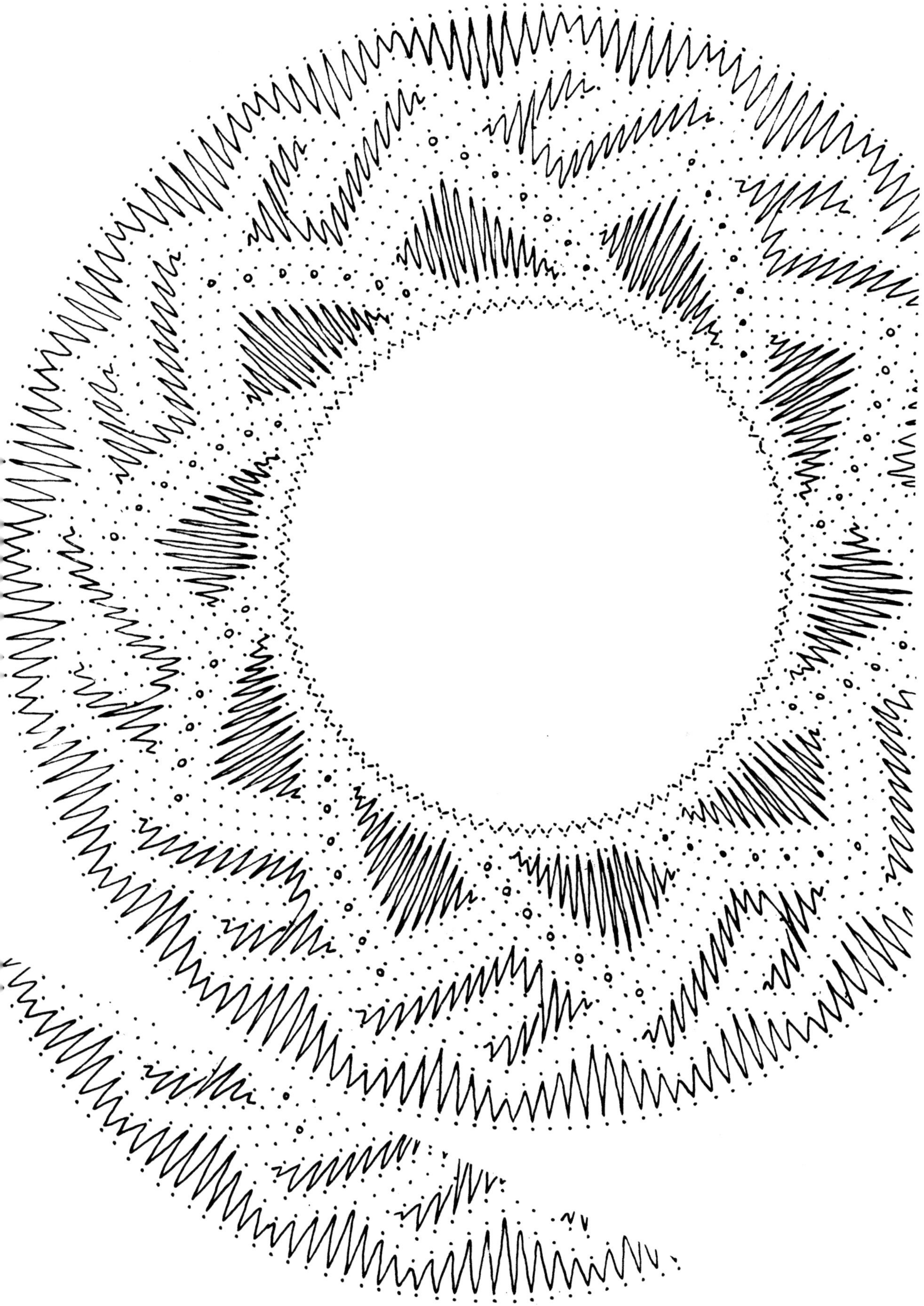

89 Pattern for fig. 87

2) Japanese

In another example of an oriental pattern (fig. 90), taken from the same source book, a secondary trail has been added to the resultant lace design (fig. 93), to fill in the space left by the main trail. This second trail has been worked in a second colour, but could be worked in half-stitch (figs 91 and 92).

90 Second Japanese border pattern

91 Detail of fig. 92

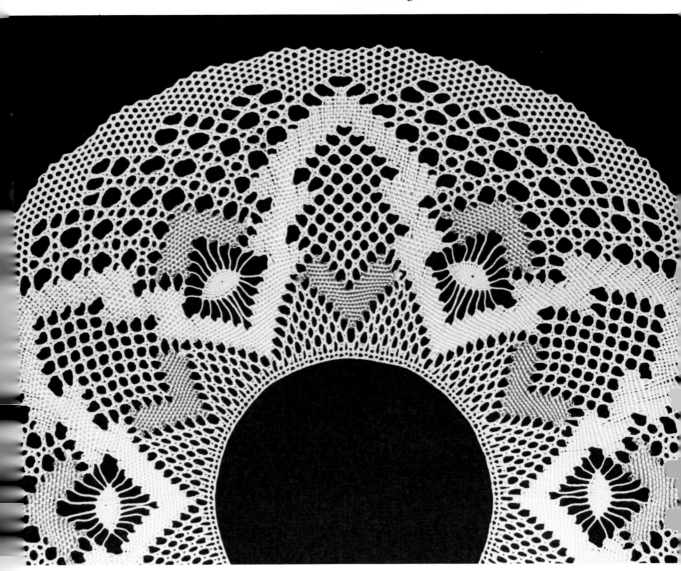

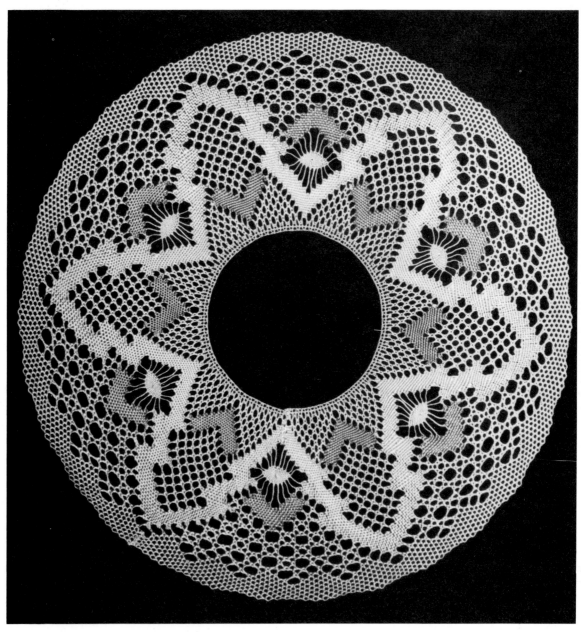

92 Interpretation in white and grey 300/4 silk,
for insertion in a circular silver tray. 38 pairs

93 Pattern for fig. 91

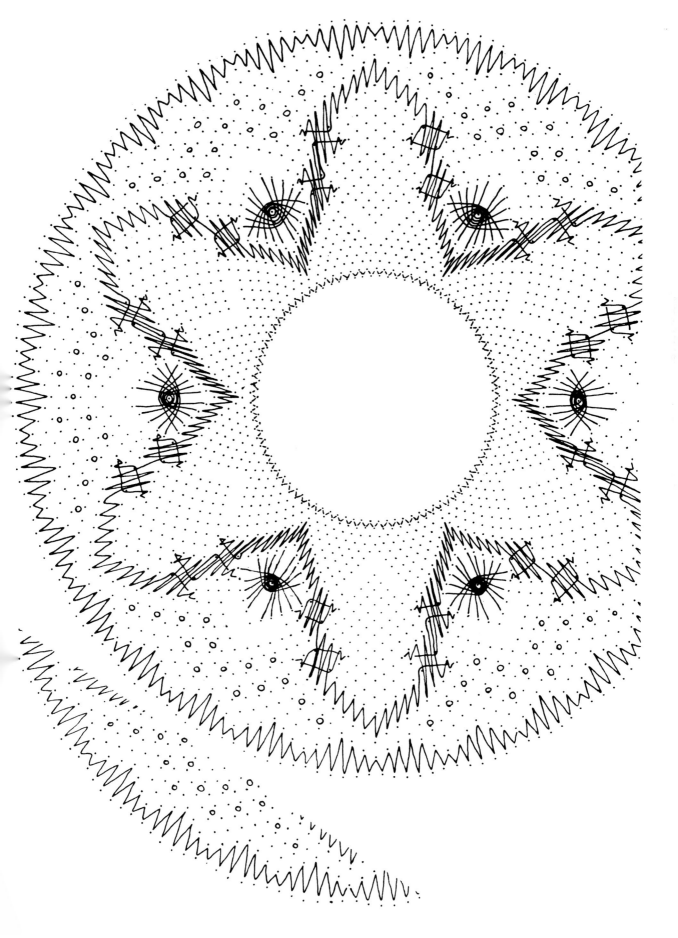

3) *Art Deco runner*

An Art Deco pattern (fig. 94) has been taken from the same book which supplied the shape for the necklace in Chapter Seven. The pattern has been

94 Art Deco pattern

made up as a runner (figs 95, 96 and colour plate 3), but complementary square mats to turn the project into a duchess set can be drafted by reflecting the end.

A few words of caution, however. Many of the best old laces, like Chantilly and Bucks, were produced by joining small sections to make large areas, and it may seem sensible to suggest that this runner could be worked down one side and then up the other with sewings in the middle, keeping the foot in place with a pair of passives which would be removed as work proceeded up the other side. However, the single twist placed before and after the pin *disappears* at each sewing! How would you tackle this problem?

It was the Dutch lace designer J.J. Vandenhorst who pointed out that two twists always disappear if you run a pair out and round a pin with no foot to keep it in place – you need four or five twists at each pin. The most aesthetically successful method of doing this runner may well have been to use twice the number of bobbins and make it all in one piece, but it still seems clear that narrow laces, joined if necessary, are easier and quicker to complete than wide ones, because of the number of bobbins involved.

95 Runner end, worked in pink 16/1 Bockens Lingarn. 40 pairs used

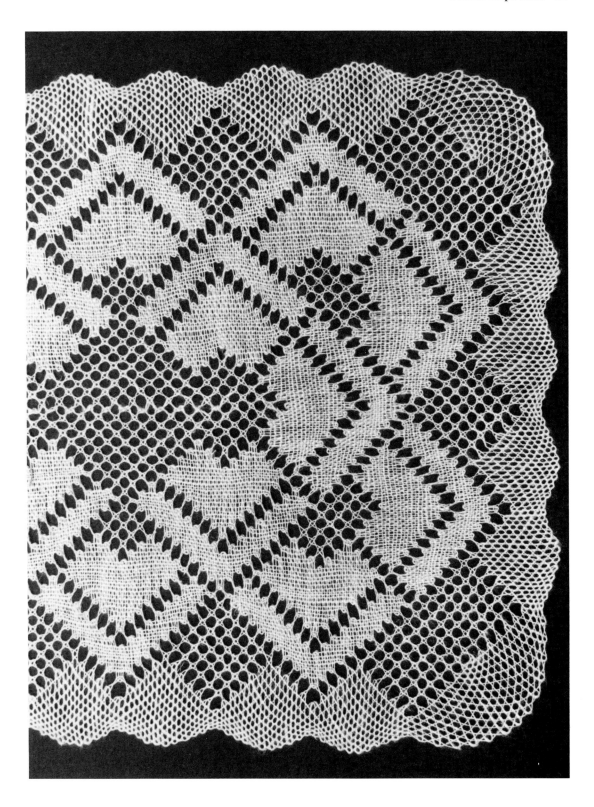

96 Pattern for runner – the end, mirrored,
provides the pattern for square mats to complete
a duchess set

4) Art Deco border

97 Art Deco border pattern

An Art Deco motif (fig. 97) translated best into a circular mat (fig. 99) – it needed to be drawn over quite a fine grid to be effective, after proving a failure as a $\frac{1}{10}$ in scale yard-lace. This pattern has also been made several times for different purposes and with varying interpretations, and proved that curved trails look best in half-stitch (fig. 98 and colour plate 4).

98 Circular mat in two shades of pink DMC *fil à dentelles*. Made by Betty Wilson. 38 pairs

99 Pattern for Art Deco ma

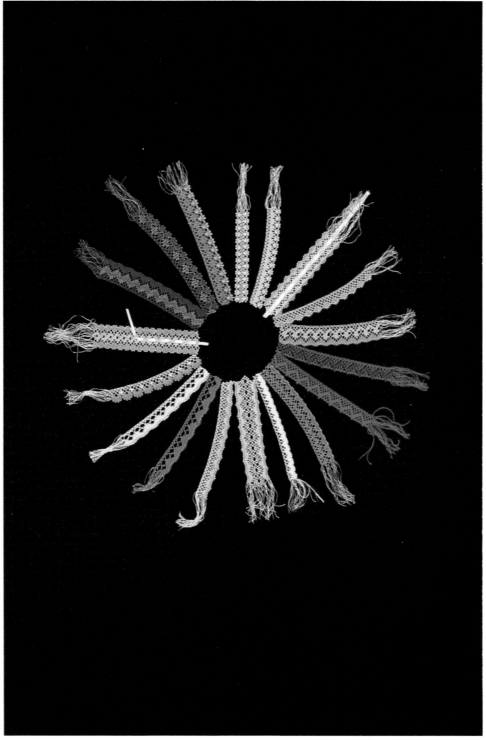

5 The ideal place to experiment with colour and stitch effects is in miniature, with fine baby laces. Most are in Mettler 30 embroidery thread, except for one tiny pattern in white 300/4 and 90 denier Piper silk

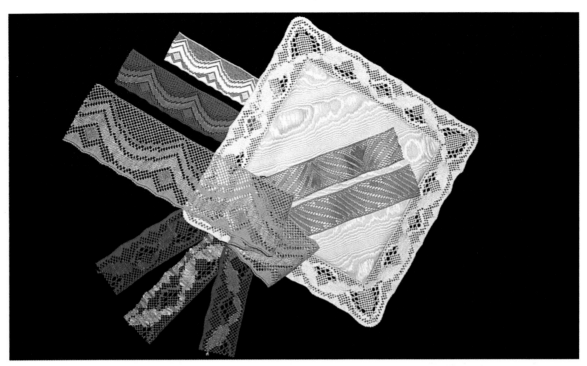

6 Variety, colour and texture can be added in different ways. The cushion cover trim from Chapter Three has been repeated (bottom right) in 16/1 Bockens Lingarn mixed with (left to right) Raffene, Yarnworks Potpourri and Berger du Nord wool/linen. The swag pattern (top right) from Chapter Eight, works equally well in dainty white 90 denier and 300/4 silk, bright Gutermanns silk, and weaving linen mixed with Filpucci Graffio. The blue and grey log patterns are in 300/4 silk

7 Coloured linen makes up thoroughly practical household laces which can be cleaned **ad infinitum**

100 Greek key pattern from another book of the Art Deco period

5) Art Deco Greek key insertion

Based on a familiar Greek key border (fig. 100), the design for the lace pattern (fig. 101) started with the use of honeycomb grid for the central area (to give a light appearance), on which the pattern elements were aligned. Combining this with rose ground for the outer areas gave a pattern that is harmonious and balanced. It made a useful insertion (fig. 102), which was applied along one edge of a table place mat (see colour plate 7). In the next chapter, there are edging and coaster patterns to match. A matching circular mat (figs 103 and 104) uses one small but distinctive part of the pattern.

101 Pattern from Greek key design

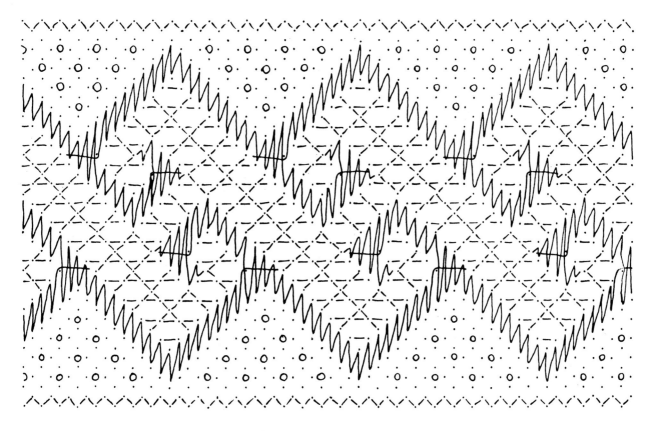

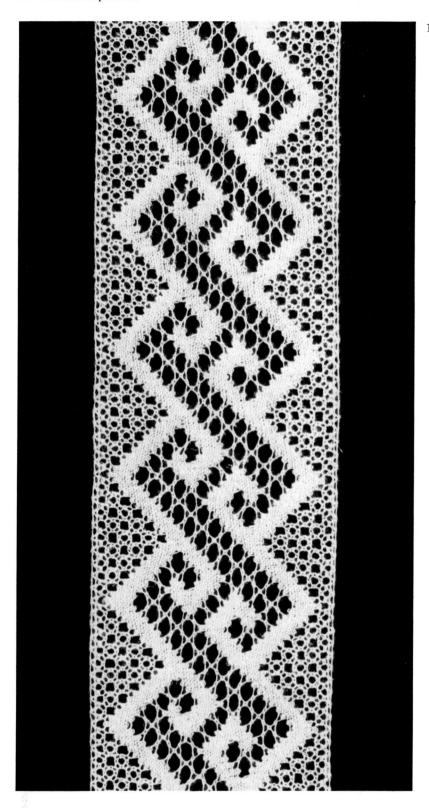

102 Lace made up in
Bockens Lingarn
16/1, blue, 44
pairs

103 Circular mat to match. 25 pairs

104 Pattern for circular mat

105 Pueblo Indian mat pattern

6) Pueblo Indian

Another pattern could also be classed as 'Greek key' but comes from a quite different continent, which shows that similar patterns can emanate from different cultures. The motif (fig. 4) comes from a Pueblo Indian pot.

This was an easy mat to draft (fig. 105), once having found suitable proportions which would repeat evenly. The lacemaker who made it up (fig.

106) wanted to make it in red, in a thread of similar weight to DMC *coton perlé* 12 which, unfortunately, is no longer produced in bright colours. Since we had not discovered Bockens cotton at that point, a ball of perlé was dyed in Dylon cold water dye, Mexican red (see colour plate 4).

106 Mat made up in DMC *coton perlé* 12 (dyed), by Lin Allen. 35 pairs

7) Celtic Interlaces – see *Geometric Patterns and Borders* by David Wade (pub. Wildwood House, 1982)

David Wade's book is particularly useful in that it provides a wealth of patterns on square and hexagonal grids. This is a very helpful feature because it aids you in keeping good proportions in your patterns.

Amongst the patterns featured are plaits, which make interesting Torchon patterns and can be made up of three, four, six or even more trails (fig. 107). However, the more you use, the greater may be the confusion of the final pattern. A pattern using only four trails (figs 108 and 109) drafted on a polar grid, gives a strong overall swirl of pattern. The lace was made up to accentuate this, in only half and whole stitch. Experimentation on paper, using the idea of following each trail in a different stitch, proved that this would grow too confusing.

107 Celtic interlaces, with three, four and six bands intertwining

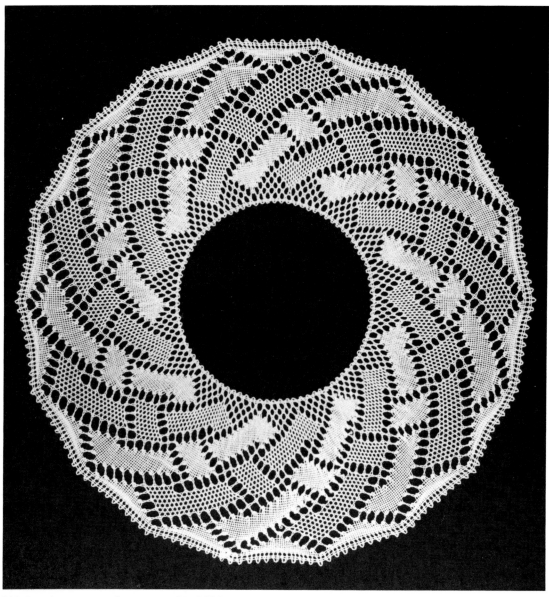

108 Interlace mat, made in cream DMC *fil à dentelles* by Betty Wilson. 36 pairs

109 Pattern for interlace mat

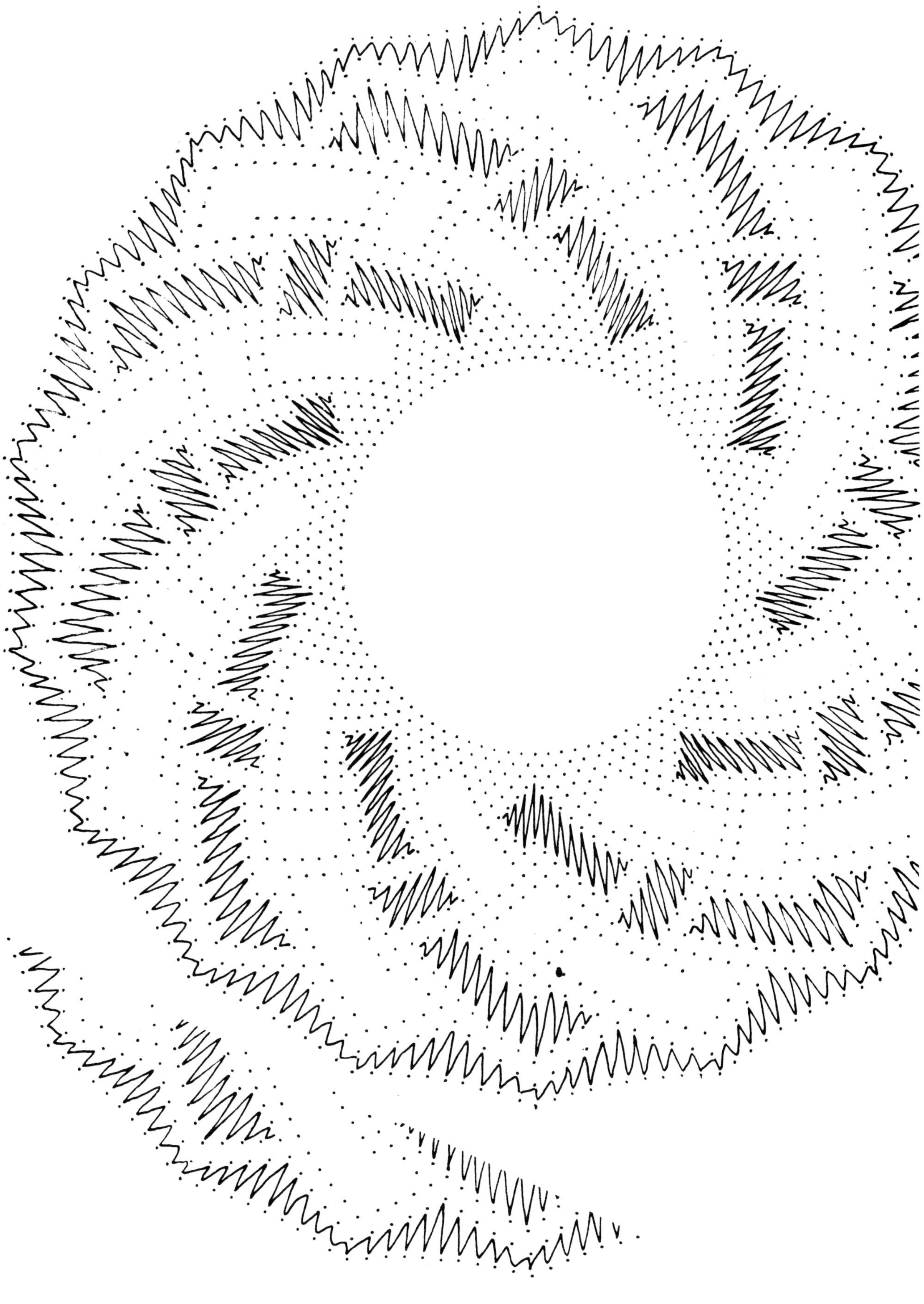

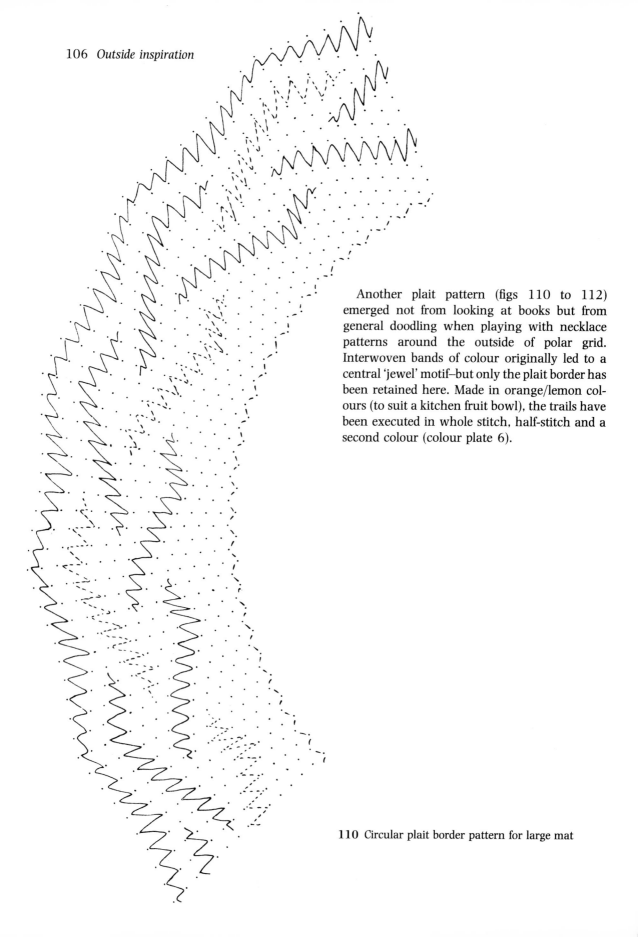

Another plait pattern (figs 110 to 112) emerged not from looking at books but from general doodling when playing with necklace patterns around the outside of polar grid. Interwoven bands of colour originally led to a central 'jewel' motif–but only the plait border has been retained here. Made in orange/lemon colours (to suit a kitchen fruit bowl), the trails have been executed in whole stitch, half-stitch and a second colour (colour plate 6).

110 Circular plait border pattern for large mat

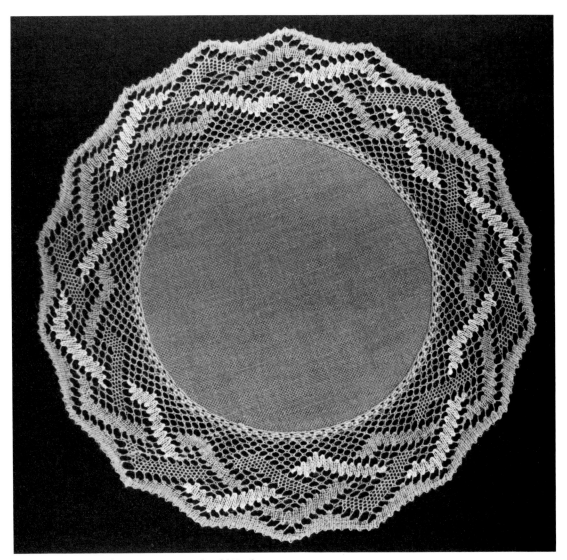

111 Large mat made up in russet and gold Bockens
Lingarn 16/1. 30 pairs

112 Detail of circular mat

8) Congo tablecloth

For Torchon, you will be looking for patterns with a strong diagonal flavour. The Congo shape (fig. 113) is an all-over pattern, but dissects well into horizontal elements to make a border pattern.

The idea then grew that one could link several borders back together to make a table-cloth.

113 All-over pattern from the Congo

114 Table-cloth centre, worked in Swedish linen 40/2, by Sarah Weaver. 50 pairs

115 (over) Table-cloth patterns: five sections overlap to produce one eighth of the pattern. Section (a) centre motif, bottom right-hand corner

116 (over) From fig. 115; (b) second and third rows, central turnover

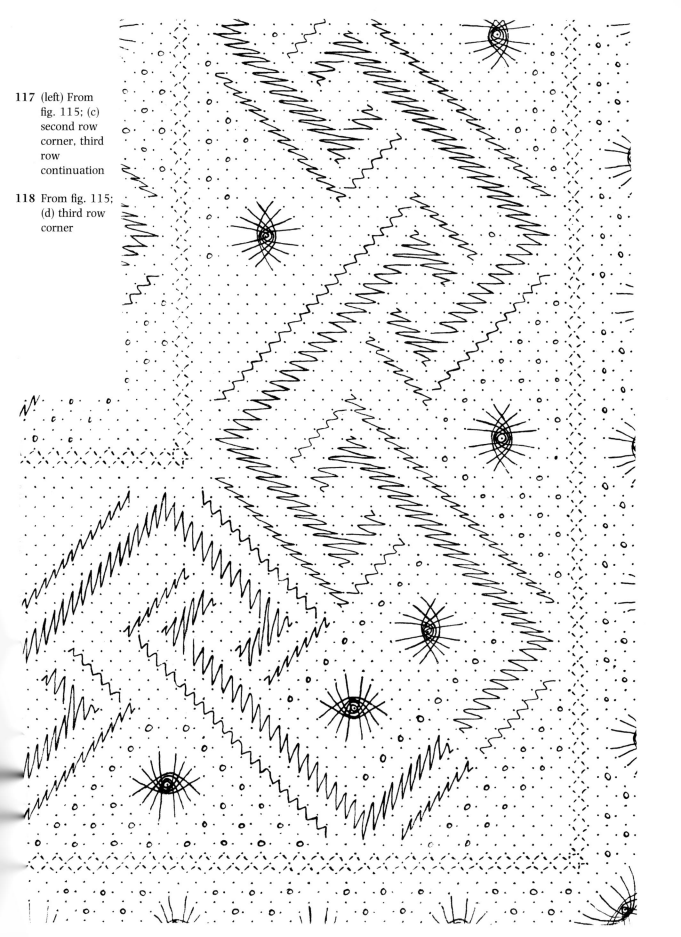

117 (left) From fig. 115; (c) second row corner, third row continuation

118 From fig. 115; (d) third row corner

119 From fig. 115; (e) outer edging, corner

Many table-cloth patterns 'grow' from the inside out, the pattern being adapted to fit each successive row. This means they are not very versatile, but it seemed useful to provide a pattern (figs 114 to 119) where a simple pricking would allow maximum choice of interpretation. The only change on each row is the addition of one extra pattern repeat: the shapes at corner and row centre remain the same. Pattern repeats may be added to the centre itself to start the cloth as an oblong, and in whatever size you want to make it, from square side-table to refectory table, you always have a pattern to fit.

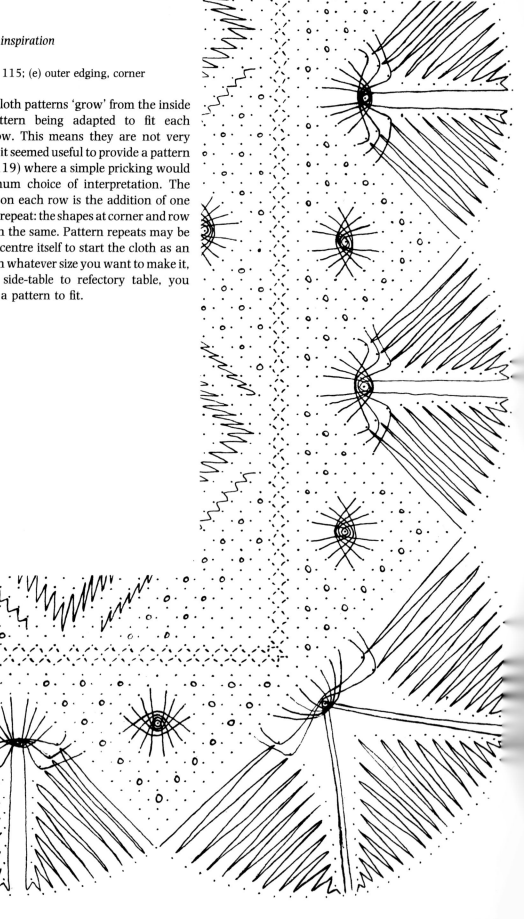

However, the edging given here fits around a square cloth with a centrepiece and two outer rows of pattern. You will need to design different edges to fit other shapes.

You can emphasize the joins with quite a heavy foot, or you can suppress them by using the extra twists discussed earlier in relation to the Art Deco runner. Sewings may be made as you work each successive row, or the separate pieces may be stitched neatly together when finished.

The pattern was originally drafted out on a large sheet of graph paper, and areas of rose ground were included to obscure the joins. You may wish to leave the rose ground out, as it has been altered slightly in each row, but it does enhance the overall effect.

It may not be easy to draft a large pattern where each successive row repeats exactly – the trick is to make sure the *depth* of the pattern (foot to foot) is *narrower* than the width of the pattern repeat. In fact, the pattern used here had to be made narrower than originally intended.

9) North American Indian Designs by Eva Wilson (British Museum Publications, 1984).

This book is a rich source of geometric patterns which cry out to be used for lace. North American readers will have such inspiration at their finger-tips. The basket pattern (figs 120 to 122) seemed a good way of utilizing the 'swirl' effect which is apparent on polar grid. The only problem in a pattern this wide is the choice of thread, which must accommodate a wide variation in dot spacing. Extra twists will firm up the honeycomb as the dots get wider apart.

120 North American Indian basket weaving

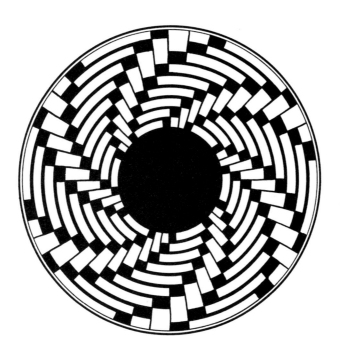

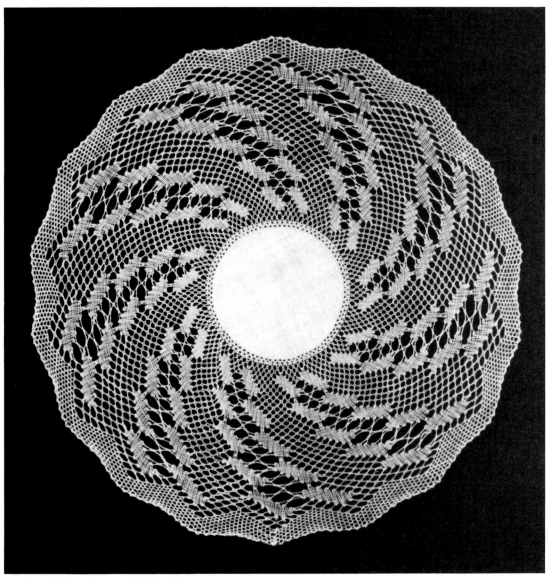

121 Mat made up in Swedish linen 80. 53 pairs

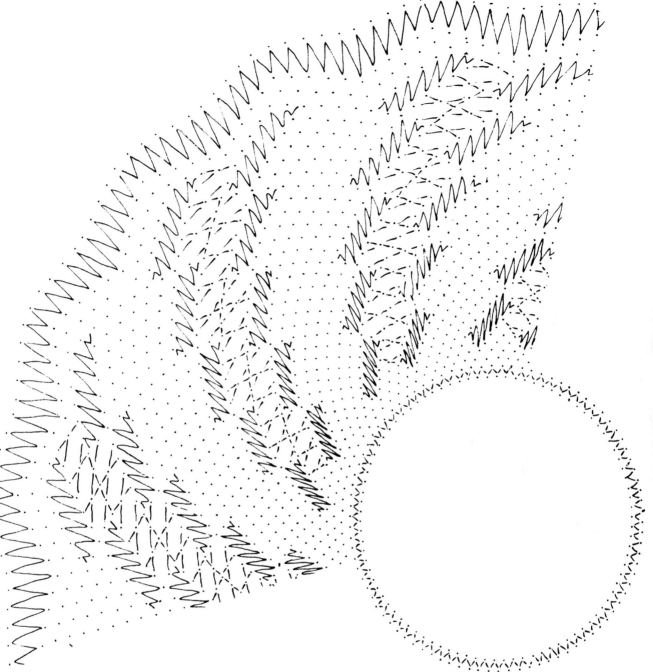

122 Pattern for 'basket' mat. One third of the pattern – the central dots are your guide for matching up the other traced or copied two thirds

Art History Books

1) Roman Pavements

Like Celtic interlace patterns, mosaic motifs offer
plenty of scope, with the added interest of using
two or more parallel trails to imitate the shading
of the tesserae. Such a pattern (figs 123 and 124)
was taken from Woodchester Roman pavement
in Gloucestershire. This is only uncovered for
viewing every decade or so, but pictures of this
and many other similarly fascinating and useful
pavements may be found in the Shire
Archaeology series's *Romano-British Mosaics* by
Peter Johnson.

123 Woodchester mosaics inspired this pattern,
made in DMC *fil à dentelles* by Betty Wilson.
55 pairs

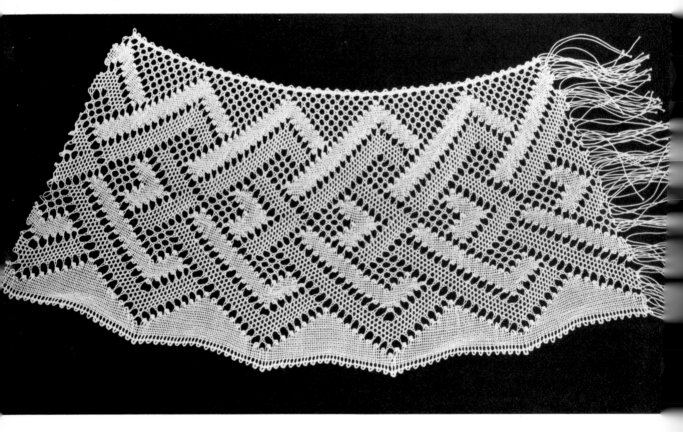

124 Pattern for mosaic circular edging. Forty pattern repeats make a circle, with interior diameter 14½in (369mm), outside diameter 23in (584mm)

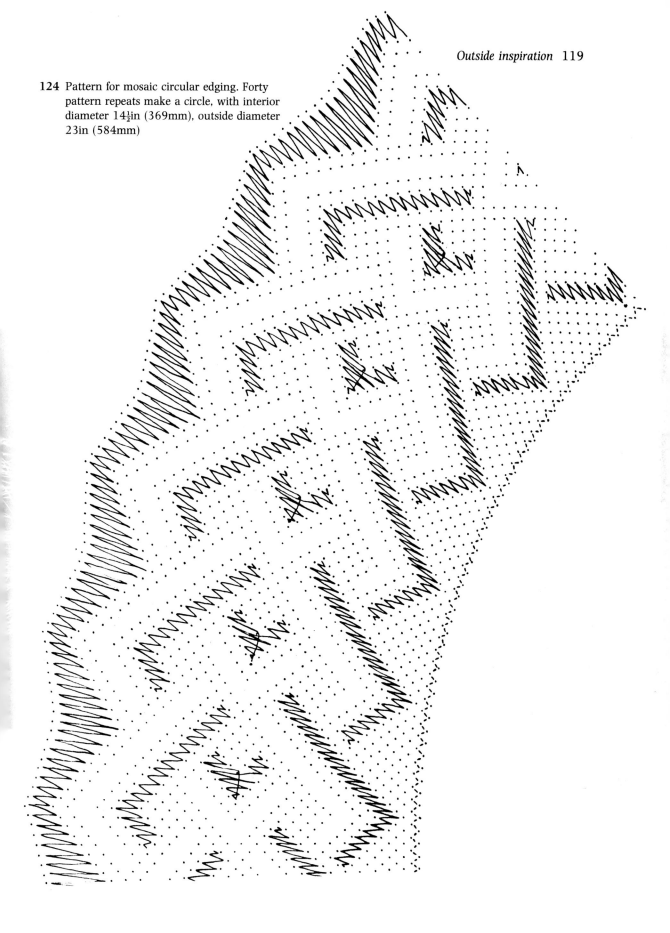

Littlecote, near Hungerford, provided a further pattern based on Roman pavement (figs 125 and 126). This had already been translated into embroidery in the eighteenth century, which is featured in Lanto Synge's *Antique Needlework* (Blandford Press). It has the advantage of a ready-made corner – a rare treat!

125 Littlecote corner and edging, made up in 40/2 Swedish linen. 49 pairs

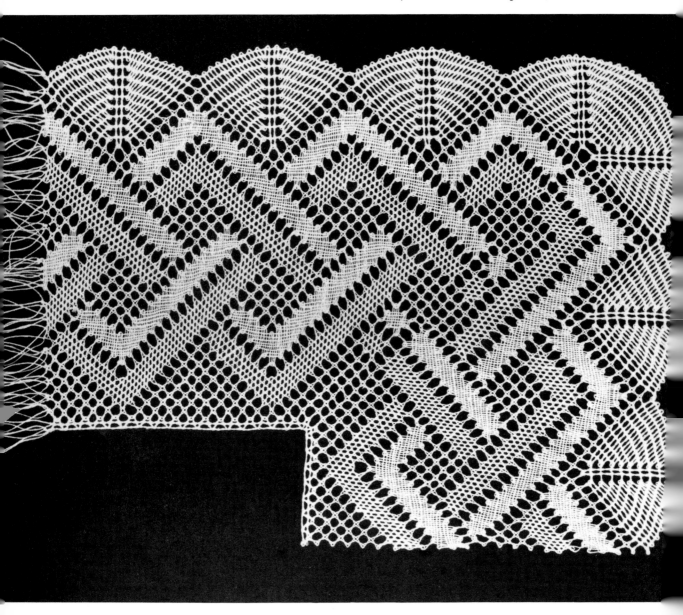

126 Pattern for
Littlecote edging

2) Hittite stone carving

A Hittite motif (fig. 127) has been used here for a straight yard-lace (figs 128 and 129) and for a circular mat (figs 130 and 131); the latter illustrates how the pattern becomes more fluid when drafted on polar grid.

The irregular head was not difficult to draft – if one excludes the central dot that falls between each head, it will be found that there are an uneven number of dots in the inner row, and one more in the outer row.

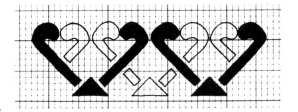

127 The original inspiration for this shape came from a small photograph of a Hittite stone carving in *The Birth of Greek Art* by Ekrem Akurgal (Methuen, 1966)

128 Corner made up in Campbells linen 50 by Betty Wilson. Extra tallies could have been worked across the corner, to increase uniformity, we decided. 36 pairs

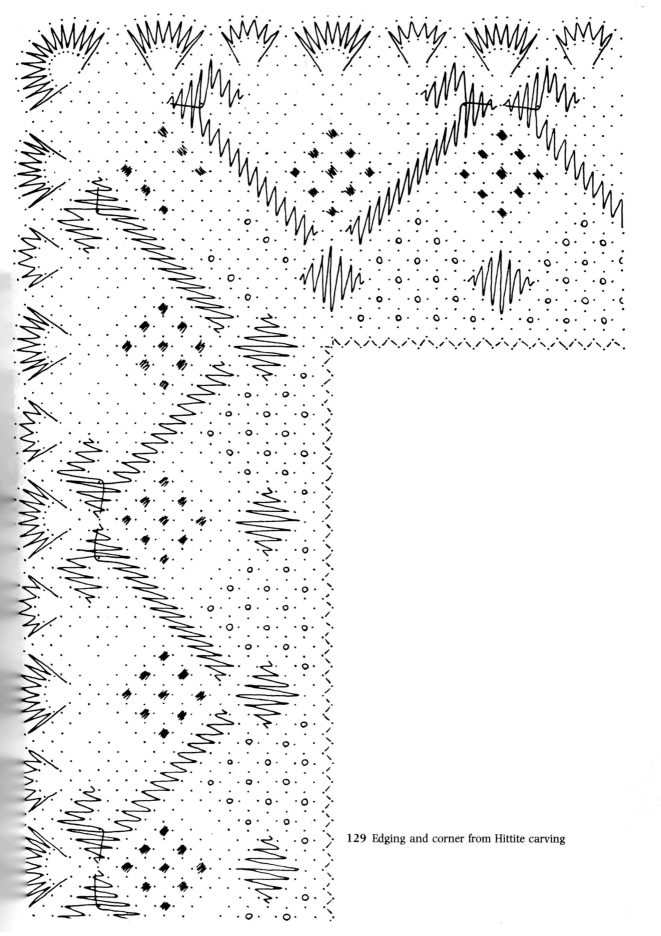

129 Edging and corner from Hittite carving

130 Circular mat from Hittite shape

131 Circular mat made up in DMC Cordonnet 100
by Betty Wilson. 31 pairs

3) UZBEK camel trappings

Asian weavers, carpet makers and embroiderers offer many interesting geometric patterns for you to use. The lace pattern eventually achieved here (figs 136 and 137) came in a rather roundabout fashion, however.

a) A simplified version of the original motif was drawn up (fig. 132).

132 Stages in the creation of 'Uzbek' edging: stage (a)

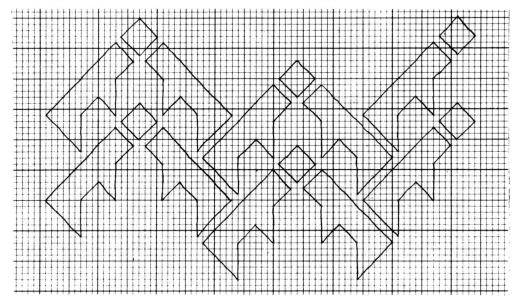

b) The area *between* the motifs was explored (fig. 133), since in themselves they were not particularly beautiful. This was a vertical pattern, which it had been decided to make into a horizontal one.

133 Stage (b)

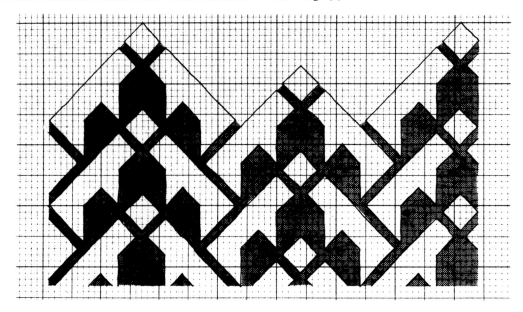

c) The new shape looked better upside down!
(fig. 134).

134 Stage (c)

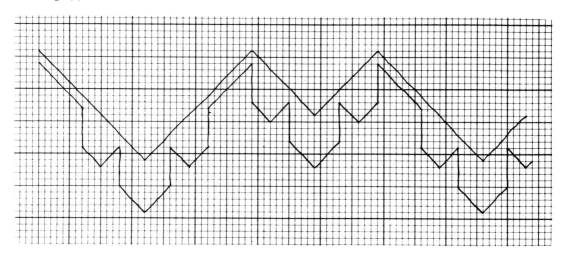

d) The motifs emerging were reminiscent of
medieval trimmings, and were arranged so that
they appeared to hang from an uneven zig-zag
band (fig. 135).

135 Stage (d)

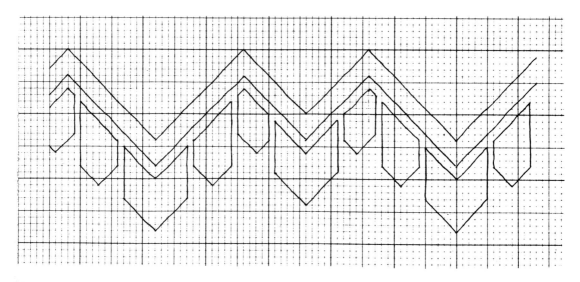

e) Extra spacing was needed, so not to crowd the shapes in the final pattern (fig. 136).

136 Stage (e) the final pricking, on 2mm grid reduced once

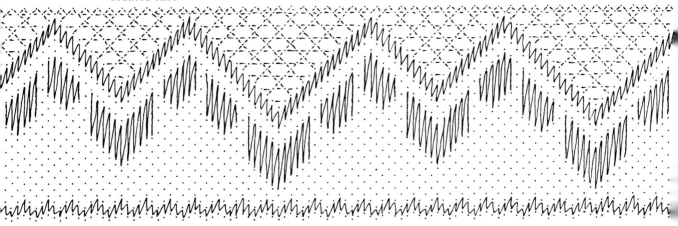

The pattern that emerges bears little relation to the original one. After all, we are not seeking to copy, faithfully, just to take ideas which we can use in some way that suits us.

The sample has been worked in white for ease of photography, but works well in pastel shades, where the sheen of 300/4 silk in the trail can give a subtle change of texture. Drafted on a $\frac{1}{10}$ in grid, this pattern also works well in 16/1 coloured linen and 40/3 spun silk.

137 Uzbek edging made in Piper spun silk 80 with 300/4 silk in the trail. 36 pairs

Magazines

During the research for this book, I found myself impressed by Post-Revolution Russian art and design, a marvellously vigorous and colourful field. I was particularly struck by the symbolic use of everyday items – not only the ubiquitous hammer and sickle, but also little factories, aeroplanes, tractors, spanners, cog-wheels and light-bulbs, worked into embroidery, crochet and printed textiles, to the glory of their combined labour.

It seemed obvious that we, too, should try to use the things around us at work and at home as pattern inspiration. Since nothing could be more

138 The cover of this electronics magazine offered a useful shape

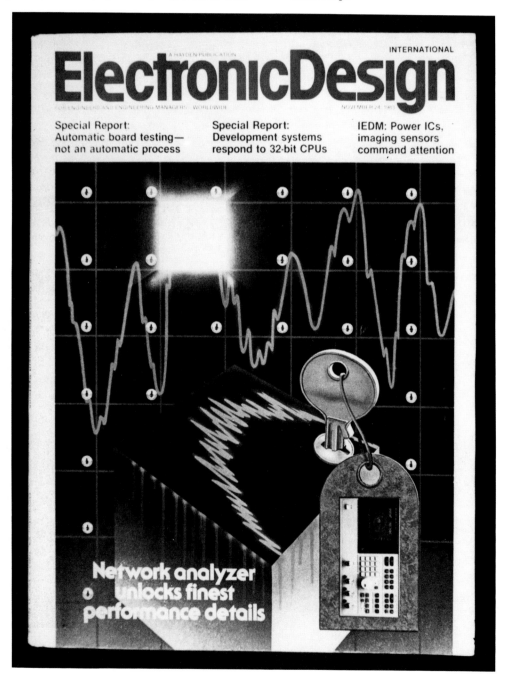

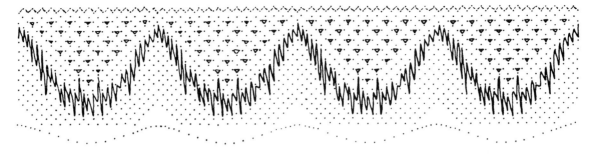

139 Pattern from electronics, drafted on $\frac{1}{10}$ in graph paper, then reduced twice on the photocopier

140 Made-up pattern of 'computer' lace –
120 BOUC linen with Klippans lingarn gimp.
33 pairs plus gimp

up-to-date than electronics, the field in which my husband works, I started scanning his trade magazines for inspiration, and quickly found 'Electronic Design' (fig. 138).

The motif was simple to draw up on graph paper. The upper area was then filled with triangular ground, to make it dense, while the edge area was made as light as possible (fig. 139). The motif was then worked with one gimp, because that was all there was room for (fig. 140).

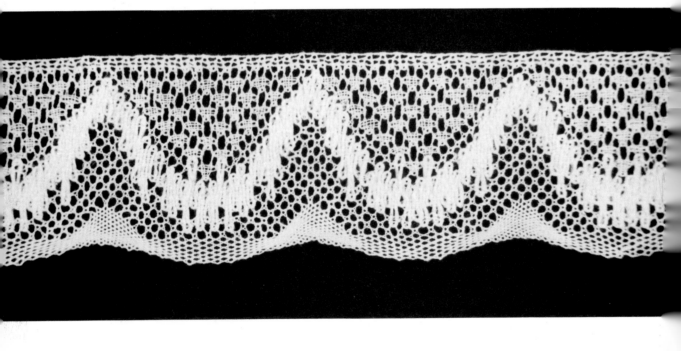

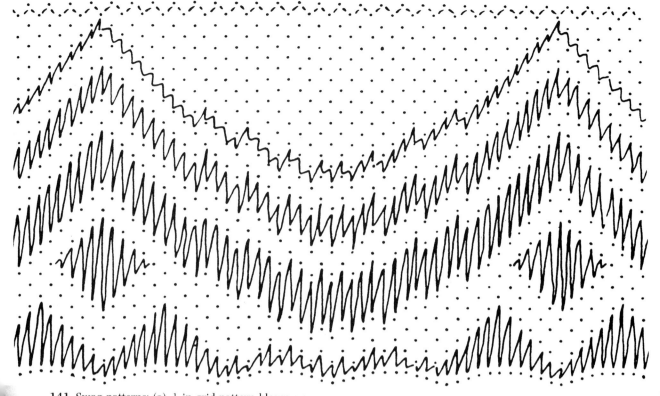

141 Swag patterns: (a) $\frac{1}{10}$ in grid pattern blown up once on the photocopier

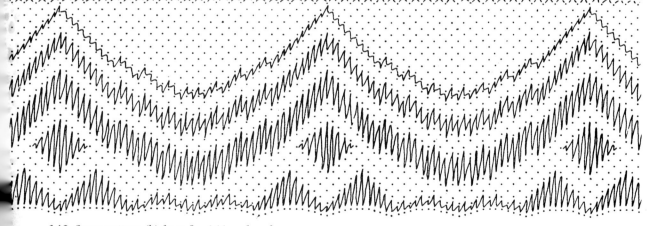

142 Swag pattern (b) from fig. 141, reduced once

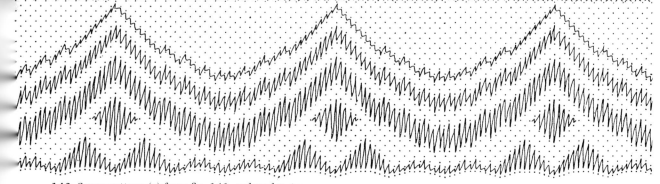

143 Swag pattern (c) from fig. 141, reduced twice

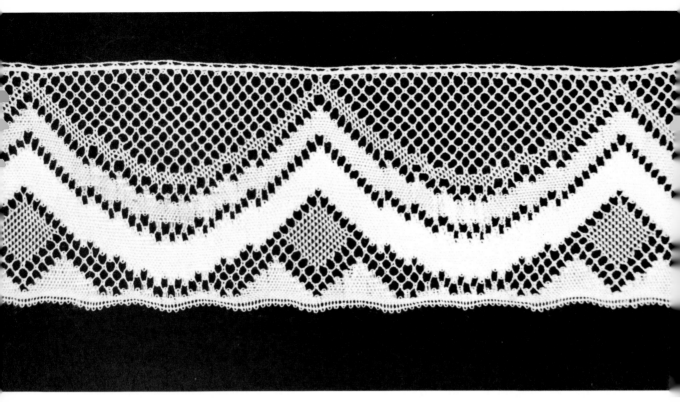

144 Smallest swag pattern, made up in 90 denier Piper silk, with the lower trail in 300/4 silk. 38 pairs

The swag patterns (figs 141 to 144) are rather similar in shape, so have been included here. The pattern was drafted as a vehicle for several different coloured threads – one each in the trails, a fourth in the edge, and a fifth as body colour (see colour plate 6). It can also be made with just one contrast thread in the lower trail, and in various different sizes. (The largest version, for furnishing use, was made in 16/1 linen and Filpucci Graffio.) *After* I had designed this pattern, I spotted it in a magazine – it had been interpreted in a slightly different way a hundred years before by Victorian machine lacemakers, proving that there is nothing new under the sun.

9 | Solving problems

In the patterns considered so far, we have not had to concern ourselves too much with restricting the eventual size of the lace; we have tended to allow the appearance of the pattern to dominate. Sometimes this is not practical as you may have to make your piece of lace a certain size – for example to fit frames or coasters. In such circumstances, you may find yourself, quite literally, in a tight corner where every dot counts.

On the other hand, you may be frustrated by a pattern that is just not quite right for the project in mind. Perhaps you want to make a 16in place mat, but the pattern repeat of the edging you have chosen is one-and-a half inches, which allows you full repeats at 15in or 16½in. The only answer to this problem is to decide on the repeat needed first, and then set about designing the pattern. This involves fitting pattern elements into the space you have allowed yourself, and is not too difficult with a little practice. For example, an edging (figs 145 and 146) to match the Greek key insertion shown earlier, required an accurate pattern repeat every one inch to suit the place mat which was trimmed with the lace.

146 Pattern made up in 16/1 blue linen, and applied to place mat. 14 pairs

To make a coaster to match the place mat, it was necessary to modify the Greek key pattern to fit. As was explained in the previous chapter, an interesting part of the pattern had already been turned into a circular mat (fig. 103), but when a friend suggested we heat-seal it on to a commercially produced cork coaster, it proved the wrong size.

There was very little room to do more than give a flavour of the pattern, but it does fit, both in size and style (figs 147, 148, and colour plate 7). For heat-sealing, there has to be a gap between the edge of the lace and the edge of the mat, leaving even less space to play with – we have to do the best we can.

For a slightly smaller coaster, the problems can be broken down in this way:

∗ Draw round the coaster to find its size.

∗ Draw a smaller circle inside to leave room for the heat sealing.

∗ Define an edging, and see how much room is left for a pattern – it may be very little!

145 Pattern with 1in (26mm) repeat featuring cloth stitch and rose ground to complement Greek key pattern

147 Lace mats heat-sealed under plastic on to cork
or cork-based coasters. One worked in blue
linen (top, 18 pairs), the other in russet linen
with central motif in copper thread (15 pairs)

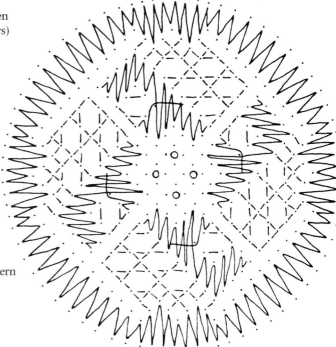

148 Pattern for coaster to match Greek key pattern

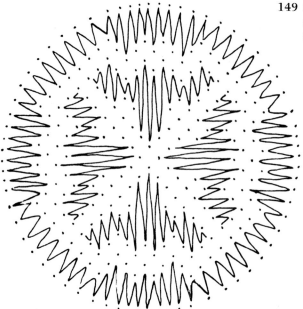

149 Suggested pattern for smaller coaster, with central motif which could be made in contrast thread

The best solution (fig. 149) seemed to be a simple shape in a contrasting thread, but this still leaves plenty of scope for interpretation in virtually any two colours or textures that take your fancy. Part of the problem with the above exercises was that they were based around a thick thread. It would be much easier to use finer grid and thread. With plenty of space left round the lace, and a coloured backing to match the table decor, the result can be most attractive.

There are many items made for lace inserts – pot-lids, key rings, door finger plates, trays, and all manner of frames. They are not difficult to fill, with a bit of thought. Define the space you have to fill; decide on the thread and the grid you want to use; choose an edging; and then play in the space you have left.

Sometimes, things can get more complicated. The 'Klipframe' is sold in most art shops, is very cheap, and makes a cheerful present with a photograph in the centre surrounded by a lace edging. Glass is held to the backing only by small clips, so there is no other frame to compete with the lace. Unfortunately, the proportions of the top and the side of the A5 size chosen for my example did not match – the top is 5.4 in (138mm) and the side is 7.8in (198mm). Only a fairly narrow

pattern was needed, since it is only a support to the main star of the piece, the picture.

Eventually, trying fan edgings of different widths, it was noticed that there were four dots too many left on the top, and seven down the side. That was more or less the same as the number of joins between the heads. Putting an extra dot between each head, and using it for a French Fan, was the best solution, and an extra dot down the side was incorporated in a large central fan. A trail beneath the heads gains an interesting wiggle, so a very simple pattern has a bit of life to it, especially if made in two colours. The final problem was that the foot would not lie absolutely straight on top of the photograph – so a small card mount was added to neaten it up (fig. 151).

150 Frame pattern to fit 'Klipframe', 15cm by 21cm (5.8 × 8.25in) (A5 size). 14 pairs

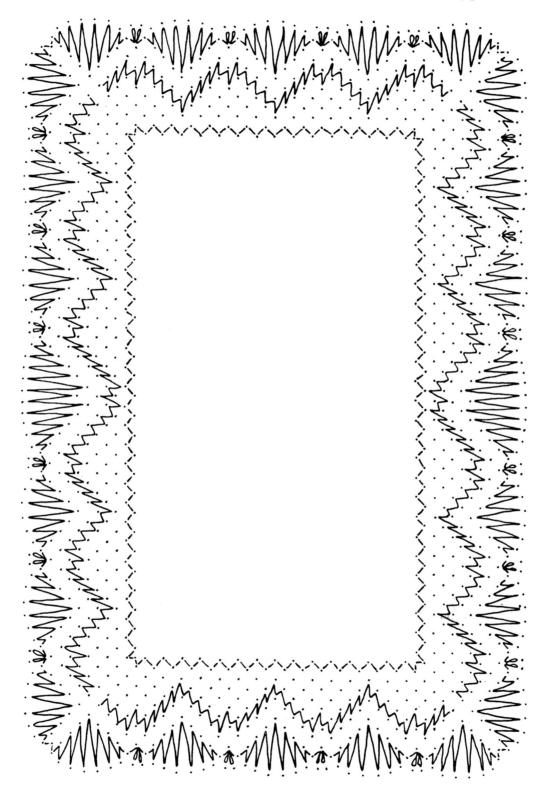

151 Lace made up in two shades ecru and gold,
of super spun silk 40/3

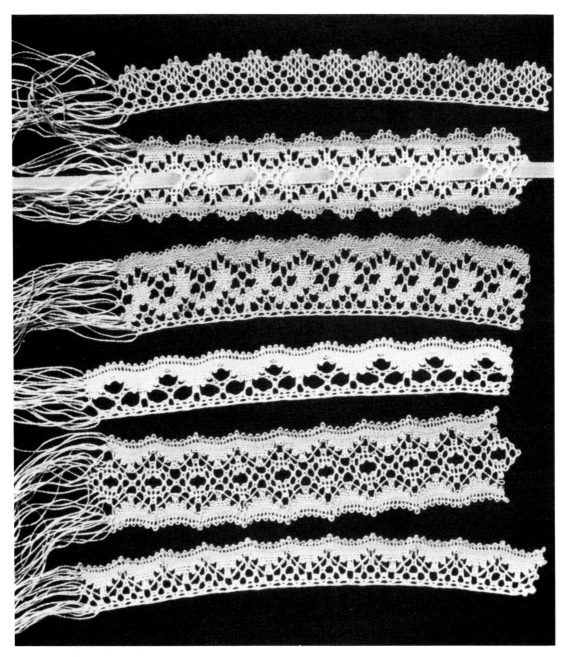

152 Little patterns for Mettler 30 machine
embroidery thread or similar fine threads:
(a) half stitch fan; (b) matching eyelet lace,
made up with the fan in whole-stitch with
worker and three passives in pastel shade,
central pairs in white; (c) wider edging with
border in darker shade than main body of lace;
(d) honeycomb edging; (e), (f) eyelet lace and
matching trim with pointed edges, with the
edges made in deeper shades outlined with one
twisted pair

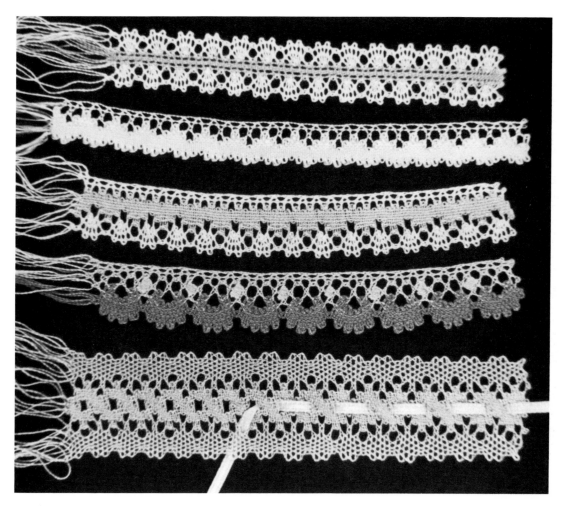

153 Little patterns: (g) French fan double edging
(ideal for applying down a seam) with outer
fans in white, central trail in pastel shade;
(h) 90 denier silk was used for the passives,
with 300/4 silk as the worker; (i) white fans,
with trail in another colour; (j) double threads
were used to emphasize the scallops, which
were made in a deeper shade than the main
passives; (k) trimming suitable for very narrow
ribbon

A problem which seemed common to a number
of friends was their inability to find enough small
patterns, fine edgings for hankies, baby clothes
and wedding items about $\frac{2}{5}$in (10mm) wide. This
is a very severe restriction! It is not just a question
of reducing a standard pattern on a photocopier.
To reduce to $\frac{2}{5}$in (10mm), the original pattern
must be no more than 1in (26mm) wide, drafted
on $\frac{1}{10}$in grid. This means a reduction of three or
four times, and the lace can then be worked in
Mettler 30 embroidery cotton, Trident 60 or Piper
90 denier silk.

You can squeeze in a variety of motifs such as
simple edgings, simple trails, eyelets for the
insertion of tiny ribbons, and small motifs like
diamonds and tallies (figs 152 to 169, and colour
plate 5).

Interest can be played up with your interpretation – this is the ideal place to experiment with
colour, to try out the theories in Chapter 3, to be
bold, subtle, courageous, restrained, all at mini-
mum cost. Combinations tried out in colour plate
5 include subtle shades of pastel and bright
complementary colours, to demonstrate that

154 Little patterns: (1) French fans made in double thread, and two workers, one in a contrast thread, in each cloth stitch diamond, with the contrast workers then taken round the half-stitch diamond as a 'gimp'; (m) the workers in the trail pop out at the edge, which has two parallel passives; (n) wider edging with trail for contrast thread; (o) narrower edging with small trail for contrast treatment

courageous combinations can often work just as well as traditional white.

One of the most difficult of all problems to solve is where to find the time needed for lacemaking. Friends who inquire, casually, whether one could make something for a bazaar cannot imagine how long it would take to make anything worthwhile. One solution, however, is to use the coloured linens and pretty textured threads, and draft simple edgings or motifs on $\frac{1}{8}$in grid, enlarge them on the photocopier, and apply the result to dainty items. It is still a labour of love, but at that scale it is possible to manufacture a simple, colourful motif in a couple of hours, and one of the eyelet patterns given above would make a fast and effective cake frill.

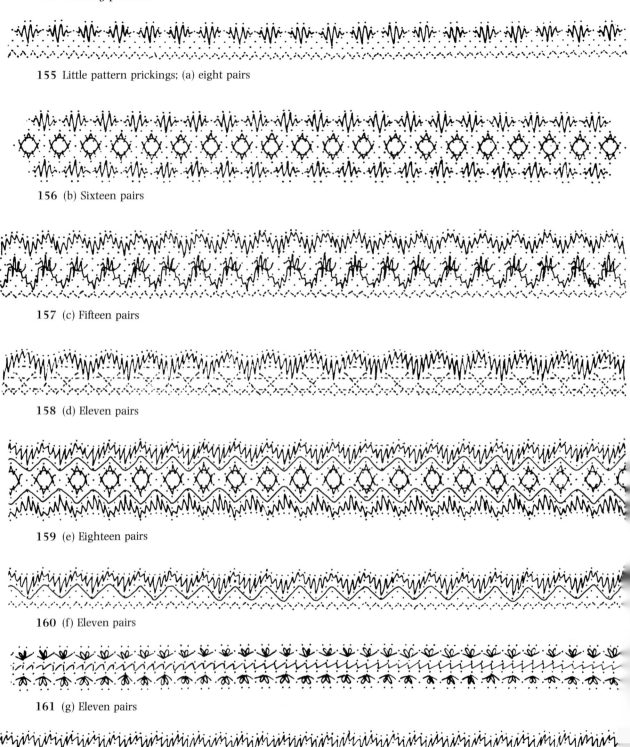

155 Little pattern prickings; (a) eight pairs

156 (b) Sixteen pairs

157 (c) Fifteen pairs

158 (d) Eleven pairs

159 (e) Eighteen pairs

160 (f) Eleven pairs

161 (g) Eleven pairs

162 (h) Up to nine pairs

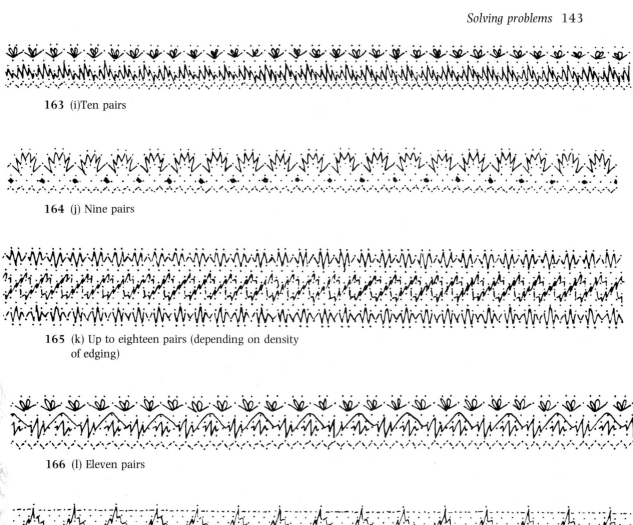

163 (i)Ten pairs

164 (j) Nine pairs

165 (k) Up to eighteen pairs (depending on density of edging)

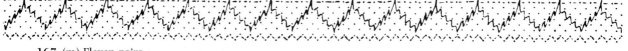

166 (l) Eleven pairs

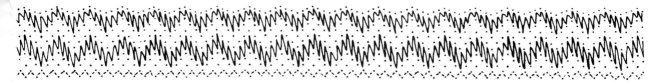

167 (m) Eleven pairs

168 (n) Fifteen pairs

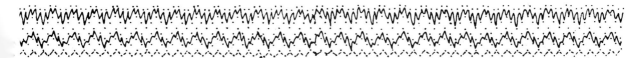

169 (o) Eleven pairs

10 | Playing with pattern

Design is a continuous process – only you know when you have achieved what you are seeking, and until you find it you have to keep working. That process may involve several people, transferring a design shape between different media, or one person altering and improving her work for her own satisfaction. This final chapter demonstrates that a piece of lace is seldom a final, complete and unalterable object: a motif may be used in many different ways.

Reconsider the lavender bag (fig. 51) which featured what one might call a 'Lazy M' shape. This appeared to offer quite an attractive trail shape, which could be expanded and improved. One corner was also made up in a different stitch to the others (all in whole stitch, instead of half and whole stitch), which suggested that it ought to be possible to design two (or more) different corners for one pattern, to allow the lacemaker a choice or a combination.

This is an entirely asymmetrical pattern. It appeared that the majority of Torchon patterns were symmetrical, with at least a turnover and a mirrored corner, so it could be more interesting to design a pattern which flowed only in one direction round the work.

A tray cloth edging (figs 170 and 171) illustrates how this was achieved. The whole and half-stitch trails flow through the corners in such a manner as to emerge capable of continuing the pattern as before – the 'Lazy M' shape starts off at the inner edge of the pattern and ends near the outer edge, so must be capable of shifting back from high to low as it works through the corner. Two variations did indeed prove possible.

Another variation would be to put a reverse in the middle of each edge, by allowing the 'M' at that point to mirror with two long legs. By mirroring

the corners, one could prick four variations from one pattern.

Perhaps it was wrong to stop the foot of the 'Lazy M' shape when for the sake of a couple of extra rows of pattern, it could have joined the next one. Hindsight is a useful tool, which can be brought into play months or years later!

The shape was transferred next into a collar pattern, but served to prove that asymmetrical shapes do not make a collar that is to everybody's liking – for the ends will not necessarily match. Most will prefer collar points that do match, unless contrast is a deliberately sought feature. So collar motifs should either be symmetrical, or capable of reverse in the centre.

The shape did work well on a circular grid, however, and was then enlarged to a circular mat about 11in across. It was allowed to be as wide as needed. The legs extended down, and interwove: being asymmetrical the whole pattern had to be drafted to prove that the legs correctly joined up with themselves. This was a most interesting exercise, and although it has been interpreted (fig. 172) in the manner in which it was drafted, the spaces could be filled with textured stitches.

170 Tray cloth edging adapted from original lavender-bag design. Made in Campbells linen 50 (which was a little too thick – 70 would have been better). 25 pairs

171 A choice of corners for the edging

172 Pattern elaborated to make wide circular
edging, made (and well used) by Jane de
Pearle, in Campbells linen 70

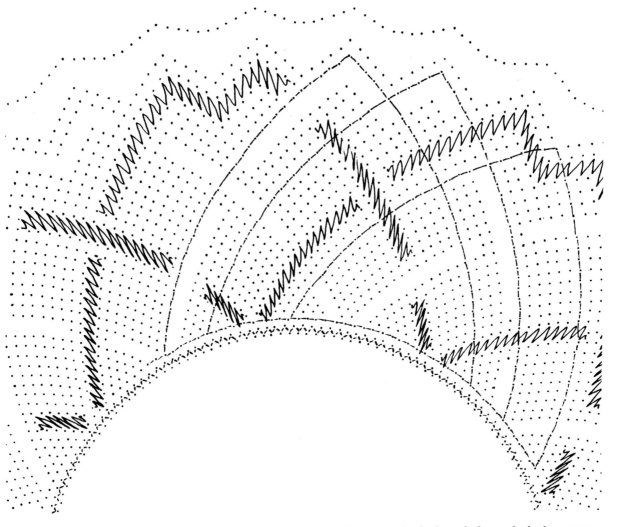

173 Section of the circular pattern, showing how scales were drawn and arranged

The double-pointed petals in themselves looked as if they had potential, and suggested overlapping scales. A large and a small scale were traced off (fig. 173) and large scales were cut in green tissue paper, while the small ones were cut from orange tissue. A sheet of tracing paper was then taped over the top of the pattern and the scales were lightly glued into position. When held before a light, or a sunny window, a most interesting series of gradations occurred (fig. 174). They appeared to shade from dark to light in 10 stages. A diagram of the resulting pattern was drawn up, and it was determined where each shade occurred.

The question of finding 10 different lace stitches to shade from light to dark then arose. Could it be achieved by variations of half and whole stitch alone? A pricking was drawn up and the idea tested (fig. 175), which proved a miserable failure. Perhaps it could be achieved with a variety of rose grounds and other simple stitches? Pamela Nottingham's books including Torchon

174 (*above right*) The tissue shapes, arranged and back-lit

175 (*below right*) First attempts at transferring shades into lace stitches. Working from left to right, three different sets of stitches were tried, in *fil à dentelles* on quadrant grid over five dots per sector

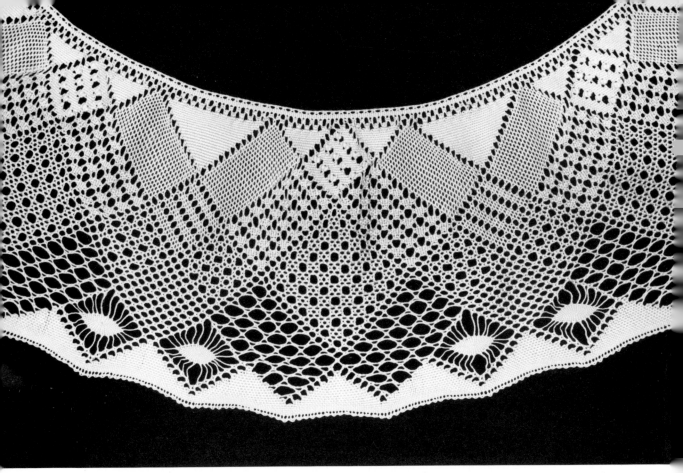

176 Final attempt at bertha pattern, drawn up on the edge of a quadrant grid, over 10 dots per segment. The stitches used included whole-stitch, whole-stitch stripes with tallies, half-stitch, half-stitch stripes, triangular ground, half-stitch rose ground, two pin rose ground, half-stitch Torchon ground, honeycomb and big spiders. 63 pairs

patterns were thumbed through, and various grounds gauged. Cook and Stott's book of stitches proved useful in sorting out minor details, and also introduced triangular ground, which proved to be the hitherto elusive medium-weight stitch needed. If you refer again to the test pattern (fig. 175), you will see that three sets of stitch changes were made, involving two prickings.

A good way to help evaluate a pattern is to hold it up against a dark background in front of a mirror – this gives you quite a new perspective. Another useful aid is someone with no knowledge of lacemaking, who will not be seduced by admiration of technique into saying a design has worked when it has not.

One problem posed itself with the rose ground – the preparatory crossing of adjacent pairs clouded the channels between each area of ground which the first, unsuccessful, attempt did at least prove to be needed for clarity. There were also an odd number of pinholes in some of the areas, making four-pin grounds, like rose ground, difficult.

The problem was filed away for several months, with a solution only becoming evident when it was enlarged to make a bertha collar. Regret that the petal shapes had never worked in an entirely satisfactory way prompted the suggestion that the pattern be redrafted in a larger scale which could include even numbers of dots in rose ground areas. An extra line of pinholes at the edges of the rose blocks could also make the channels easier to see.

This proved much easier than expected and repeated neatly over three segments of 90° polar grid (figs 176 and 177). All that remained to do was to make up 14 repeats!

If you prefer a bertha collar to have a beginning and an end, as the old ones do, you can design and

177 Pattern for bertha collar
(14 repeats) or circular
edging (12 repeats). The
marked section shows one
repeat

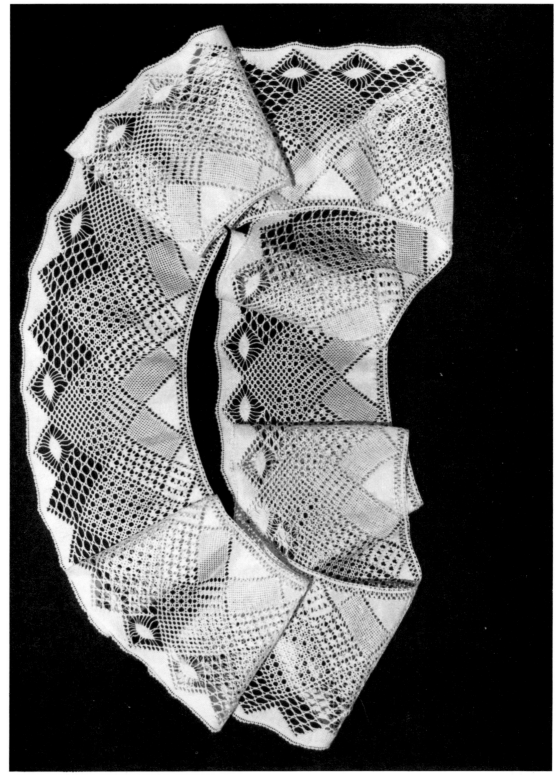

178 Bertha collar before mounting on to garment,
made up in 300/4 silk

work this like the ends of the fan in Chapter Seven (fig. 57), or provide a conventional collar edging. An opening is preferable, for there are fewer commercial dress patterns that cater for continuous neck frills than patterns with a front or back opening.

So, we started out designing lace for a lavender bag and have progressed through edgings for mats and collars. My own exercise culminated in trimming a silk cocktail dress with the lace. It was not difficult to achieve, since it was designed in a certain spirit of adventure, but it did take a considerable time. One just kept working until reasonable results were obtained.

Although the last in this book, this was, in fact, the first project to be completed. Realizing that not everyone would be able to spend the amount of time it took, this book evolved from subsequent efforts to find design short-cuts that gain quicker results.

I hope my experiences have shown that design is not just for the few: once a few basic rules are combined with your own enthusiasm, pattern play can offer practical rewards and be great fun.

References

Introduction

1. *The Technique of Bobbin Lace*, Pamela Nottingham, Batsford, 1976
2. *The Technique of Torchon Lace*, Pamela Nottingham, Batsford, 1979
3. *Torchon Lace for Today*, Jenny Fisher, Dryad Press
4. *The Book of Bobbin Lace Stitches*, Bridget M. Cook and Geraldine Stott, Batsford, 1980
5. *Practical Skills in Bobbin Lace*, Bridget M. Cook, Batsford, 1987

Chapter One

1. 'John Makepeace: Backwoods or Forwards?', Deyan Sudjic, *Crafts* magazine, May 1982
2. *Land of the Lakes*, Melvyn Bragg, Secker and Warburg, 1983
3. *Lace Making and Collecting*, A Penderell Moody, Cassell, 1909
4. 'La Stylistique dentellière a l'époque Art Nouveau, son évolution jusqu'à la première guerre mondiale', Marguerite Coppens, *Revue des Archéologues et Historiens d'Art de Louvain*, 1982
5. 'Crafts: from village hall to V & A', Leslie Geddes-Brown, *Sunday Times*, 6 April, 1986
6. 'Bobbin back into the limelight', Beryl Downing, *The Times*, 15 September, 1984
7. 'Textiles North', Peter Fuller, *Crafts* magazine, March 1982

Chapter Two

1. Anni Albers quoted in *Bauhaus, 1919–1928*, edited Bayer and Gropius, Secker and Warburg, 1978
2. *The Decorative Designs of Frank Lloyd Wright*, David A. Hanks, E.P. Dutton 1979
3. *Vers un Architecture*, Le Corbusier, 1923
4. *A Potter's Book*, Bernard Leach, Faber and Faber, 1940 (reprinted 1985)
5. 'Concerning Fundamental Design', Joseph Albers, as 1
6. *The Nature and Aesthetics of Design*, David Pye, Barrie and Jenkins, 1978
7. *Logic and Design*, Krome Barratt, George Godwin, 1980

Chapter Three

1. *The Art of Color* (condensed into paperback form as *The Elements of Color*), Van Nostrand, Reinhold, 1983
2. *The Structure of Weaving*, Ann Sutton, Batsford, 1986
3. *The Art of Weaving*, Else Regensteiner, Studio Vista, 1970

Chapter Four

1. *The Anatomy of Pattern*, Lewis F. Day, Batsford, 1887
2. *Practical Designing*, edited Gleeson White, Geo. Bell and Sons, 1899

Chapter Eight

1. H. Orrinsmith *Practical Designing*, 1899

Suppliers

United Kingdom

Alby Lace Museum
Cromer Road
Alby
Norfolk
NR11 7QE

E. Braggins & Sons
26–36 Silver Street
Bedford

Stephen Cook
'Cottage Crafts'
6 Wood Lane Close
Flackwell Heath
High Wickham
Buckinghamshire
HP10 9EP

Leonie Cox
The Old School
Childswickham
Near Broadway
Worcs
WR12 7HD

J. & J. Ford
5 Squirrels Hollow
Boney Hay
Walsall
WS7 8YS

Frank Herring & Sons
27 High Street
Dorchester
Dorset
DT1 1UP

Honiton Lace Shop
44 High Street
Honiton
Devon

D.J. Hornsby
149 High Street
Burton Latimer
Kettering
Northants
NN15 5RL

All branches of John Lewis

Lambourn Valley Cottage Industries
11 Oxford Street
Lambourn
Berks
RG16 7XS

Mace and Nairn
89 Crane Street
Salisbury
Wiltshire
SP1 2PY

The Needlewoman
21 Needless Abbey
off New Street
Birmingham

Dorothy Pearce
5 Fulshaw Avenue
Wilmslow
Cheshire

Bryn Phillips
'Pantglass'
Cellan
Lampeter
Dyfed
SA48 8JD

E. and J. Piper
Silverlea
Flax Lane
Glemsford
Suffolk CO10 7RS

Peter and Beverley Scarlett
Strupak
Hill Head
Coldwells
Ellon
Grampian

J.S. Sear
Lacecraft Supplies
8 Hill View
Sherrington
Buckinghamshire

Sebalace
Waterloo Mills
Howden Road
Silsden
Keighley
W. Yorks

A. Sells
49 Pedley Lane
Clifton
Shefford
Bedfordshire

D.H. Shaw
47 Zamor Crescent
Thruscroft
Rotherham
S. Yorks

Shireburn Lace
Finkle Court
Finkle Hill
Sherburn in Elmet
N. Yorks
LS25 6EB

Stephen Simpson
Avenham Road Works
Preston
Lancs

Christine and David Springett
21 Hillmorton Road
Rugby
Warwickshire
CV2R 5DF

Valley House Crafts Studios
Ruston
Scarborough
N. Yorks

George White
Delaheys Cottage
Thistle Hill
Knaseborough
N. Yorks

Bobbin makers

T. Brown
Temple Lane Cottage
Littledean
Cinderford
Gloucestershire

T. Parker
124 Corhampton Road
Boscombe East
Bournemouth
BH6 5NZ

Richard Viney
Unit 7
Port Royal Street
Southsea
Hants
PO5 4NP

Silk weaving yarn:

Hilary Chetwynd
Kipping Cottage
Cheriton
Alresford
Hants SO24 0PW
(If you tell her you are a lacemaker, she may be
able to supply smaller quantities, oddments of
colour, etc.)

Gutermanns 100/3 silk embroidery thread:

Doreen Holmes
39 Napier Road
Crowthorne
Berks

Bockens linen and cotton yarn:

William Hall and Co (Monsall) Ltd
177 Stanley Road
Cheadle Hulme
Cheadle
Cheshire SK8 6RF

Textured knitting yarns:

Little London Spinners
Unit 8
Home Farm Craft Workshops
Lockerley Hall
Lockerly
Near Romsey
Hants

Frames and mounts:

Doreen Campbell
'Highcliff'
Bremilham Road
Malmesbury
Wilts
SN16 0DA

United States

Berga Ullman Inc.
P.O. Box 918
North Adams
Massachusetts 01247

Frederick J. Fawcett
129 South Street
Boston
Massachusetts 02130

Frivolité
15526 Densmore N.
Seattle
Washington 98113

Happy Hands
3007 S.W. Marshall
Pendleton
Oregon 97180

Osma G. Todd Studio
319 Mendoza Avenue
Coral Gables
Florida 33134

Robin and Russ Handweavers
533 North Adams Street
McMinnvills
Oregon 97128

Some Place
2990 Adline Street
Berkeley
California 94703

The Unique and Art Lace Cleaners
5926 Delman Boulevard
St Louis
Missouri 63112

Belgium

Manufacture Belge de Dentelle
6 Galerie de la Reine
Galeries Royales St Hubert
1000 Bruxelles

Kantcentrum
Balstraat 14
8000 Brugge

West Germany

Heikina De Ruijter
Kloeppelgrosshandel
Langer Steinweg 38
D4933 Blomberg
West Germany

Brigitte Wichlei
Der Feasterladen
Berliner Strasse 8
6483 Bad Soden Salmunster
West Germany

Sources of information

The Lace Guild
The Hollies
53 Audnam
Stourbridge
West Midlands
DY8 4AE

The Lace Society
Linwood
Stratford Road
Oversley
Alcester
Warwickshire
BY9 6PG

English Lace School
Honiton Court
Rockbeare
near Exeter
Devon

The British College of Lace
21 Hillmorton Road
Rugby
Warwickshire
CV2R 5DF

International Old Lacers
Mrs Robert Riddell
P.O. Box 1029
Westminster
Colorado 80030

English Director of International Old Lacers
Mrs Susan Hirst
4 Dollis Road
London
N3 1RG

Ring of Tatters
Mrs C. Appleton
Nonesuch
5 Ryeland Road
Ellerby
Saltburn by Sea
Cleveland
TS13 5LP

Index